A HISTORY OF
NEGRO SLAVERY
IN NEW YORK

A HISTORY OF
NEGRO SLAVERY
IN NEW YORK

EDGAR J. McMANUS

Foreword by
RICHARD B. MORRIS

SYRACUSE UNIVERSITY PRESS

Copyright © 1966 by Syracuse University Press
Syracuse, New York 13244-5160

All Rights Reserved

First Paperback Edition 2001
01   02   03   04   05   6   5   4   3   2   1

The paper used in this publication meets the minimum requirements of American
National Standard for Information Sciences—Permanence of Paper for Printed Library
Materials, ANSI Z39.48-1984.∞™

ISBN 0-8156-2894-3 (pbk)

Library of Congress Catalog Card No.: 66-15741

Manufactured in the United States of America

CONTENTS

Edgar J. McManus is currently professor of history at Queens College and at the Graduate Center of the City University of New York. He holds a Ph.D. from Columbia University and a J.D. from the New York University School of Law. A member of the New York Bar, Dr. McManus has taught at the University of Oslo, the University of Canterbury in New Zealand, and the National University of Ireland in Cork. He is the author of *Black Bondage in the North,* also published by Syracuse University Press, and *Law and Liberty in Early New England,* published by the University of Massachusetts Press.

FOREWORD

It was to be the tragic heritage of slavery that its abolition created as many problems as it solved. The "peculiar institution" was so varied and complex, subserved so many different alleged economic and social needs, and bore such heavy racial overtones that we are still paying a heavy price for the misdeeds of earlier generations.

One normally associates slavery with the eleven slave states of the Confederacy, but the fact is that Union states like Maryland and Delaware were also slave states in 1861 and that, at least in a technical sense, slavery existed in New Jersey when the Civil War broke out. Nor is it generally recognized how well entrenched slavery was in New York in colonial times and how difficult it was to extirpate its vestiges.

Dr. McManus's well-researched and perceptive history of Negro slavery in New York is a timely reminder of the antiquity and dimension of the problem in one of the traditionally free states. Transplanted to New Netherland by the Dutch, slavery under Roman-Dutch law evolved quite differently from the pattern unfolding in the contemporary English plantation colonies. It did not conform to the stereotype of plantation slavery fixed in the public's mind by the traditional textbook treatments. In fact, as Dr. McManus shows, it was much closer in form to colonial white servitude. Under a system of "half-freedom" slaves could be conditionally released from bondage. This was comparable to the illegal but widely common practice of slaves hiring out to themselves, a practice which, despite the Black Codes, prevailed in many parts of the Old South in the ante-bellum period. It was a form of quasi-freedom in which the Negro dwelt in a shadow-land between slavery and freedom. Much of this quasi-freedom, as we learn from Dr. McManus's account, was ended when the English conquered New Netherland. Slavery flourished in New York under English rule. Its surprising vitality came in part from the fact that slave traders left surplus Negroes in the port of New York—and it must be borne in mind that New York merchants were conspicuous in the foreign slave trade. Slavery flourished for additional reasons: because of the scarcity of white laborers who were discouraged from emigrating to New York because of that colony's restrictive land policy, and because slave retainers in domestic service were considered by New Yorkers to be a badge of social distinction.

Enlightened men, and there were a goodly number of them, were shocked by the repression of the Negro slave, by the double standard of justice that was meted out to him. With the coming of the Revolution John Jay, ever conspicuous for his opposition to slavery, declared that unless America was prepared to free the slaves, "her prayers to Heaven for liberty will be impious." Fittingly, it was John Jay's signature as governor which was affixed to the New York law of 1799 abolishing slavery through a system of gradual manumission.

This somber but moving story is expertly told and interpreted by Dr. McManus. His terse, thoughtful, and well-researched account explains the seeming paradox of upper-class New York Federalists favoring abolition while lower-class Jeffersonian Republicans were doing everything in their power to undermine the effectiveness of the emancipation law and to render the freed Negro a second-class citizen. It was a tragic paradox, too, that under the system of slavery Negroes were trained to pursue a great variety of crafts and occupations while under the status of freedom they were virtually abandoned and systematically pauperized. This is a dark chapter in the history of the state, but it needs telling. Dr. McManus's book does more than provide information on a crucial subject. It offers understanding, and it is written in a spirit of deep compassion that cannot fail to move its readers.

RICHARD B. MORRIS
Gouverneur Morris Professor
of History

Columbia University
December, 1965

PREFACE TO THE
PAPERBACK EDITION

When this book first appeared three decades ago,
there was no general work on slavery in colonial New York.
The fragmentary accounts available barely scratched the sur-
face of what had been the largest and most important slave
system north of the Mason-Dixon line. The need for a com-
prehensive study seemed compelling, particularly in the con-
text of efforts then underway to reconstruct the neglected
history of African Americans during the seventeenth and
eighteenth centuries. Although much progress has since been
made in correcting that neglect, most treatments of New
York's "peculiar institution" have focused on particular topics
and local areas. They provide valuable and useful information
but not a conspectus of the institution as a whole. This volume
still provides the only general coverage of the subject currently available.

This book traces the origins and development of New
York's slave system from its Dutch beginnings in New Netherland to its demise and legal extinction in the late eighteenth
century. Too many books on slavery inadvertently stereotype
the slaves as a passive mass that had to be harnessed and
goaded into productivity by a white elite. This stereotype was
false everywhere, even in the plantation colonies, but particularly false in New York, where slaves were economically indis-
tinguishable from free workers. Unlike the Southern colonies
where slaves were used primarily for agricultural labor, New
York had a highly diversified slave force geared to the needs of
a mixed economy. In technical skill and versatility black work-

ers spanned the whole range of free labor. Their slave status alone set them apart from the rest of the labor force. They possessed the same skills as white workers, worked at the same tasks, and—a point that cannot be emphasized too highly—played a key role in transforming a shaky Dutch outpost into a rich and powerful state.

A note on the book's style and organization may be helpful to the reader. Dates have been left in the Old Style (Julian calendar) with split annotation for dates before March 25, 1752, when the Gregorian calendar took effect in the English colonies. Where it was possible to do so without altering the essential meaning, spelling and punctuation in quotations have been modernized for reading convenience. Abbreviations, except those in modern usage, have been spelled out, and unnecessary italics eliminated. These adjustments improve textual clarity but change nothing of substance.

Many people generously assisted in the book's preparation. I am particularly grateful to Wayne Andrews, James T. Flexner, and Albert Baragwanath. My thanks also to the staffs of the New-York Historical Society, the New York Public Library, the State Library at Albany, the Museum of the City of New York, the New York Society Library, the Easthampton Free Library, and the Columbia University Library. Their cooperation and unfailing courtesy turned what often began as tedious research into a gratifying personal experience. I want to acknowledge a special obligation to the late Richard B. Morris, whose criticism and advice played an important part in the final form of the book. Finally, and lastingly, I am grateful to my late wife, Joan Thornton McManus, whose encouragement and support contributed to the completion of the project. Whatever merit this book may have owes a heavy debt to their assistance. Its shortcomings, needless to say, are mine alone.

Queens College EDGAR J. McMANUS
City University of New York

A HISTORY OF
NEGRO SLAVERY
IN NEW YORK

I. SLAVERY IN
NEW NETHERLAND

"NEW NETHERLAND WOULD BY SLAVE LABOR
BE MORE EXTENSIVELY CULTIVATED THAN IT
HAS HITHERTO BEEN, BECAUSE THE AGRI-
CULTURAL LABORERS, WHO ARE CONVEYED
THITHER AT GREAT EXPENSE TO THE COLO-
NISTS SOONER OR LATER APPLY THEMSELVES
TO TRADE, AND NEGLECT AGRICULTURE AL-
TOGETHER."
—*Board of Audit of the West India Company,*
May 27, 1647.

ONE of the paradoxes of life in the American
colonies, where personal freedom and social mobility
were so highly prized, is that most of the population was
bound to some form of legal servitude. Bondage was the
common lot of most of the early settlers, for indentured
servitude for whites and slavery for Negroes were inte-
gral parts of the colonial labor system.[1] Both forms of
bondage were relied upon to some extent to provide the
labor essential for economic progress and development.
But slavery in particular gave the colonial labor system
its essential stability, for slavery alone was fully con-
trollable by the whites. When the supply of indentured
servants diminished, or when the indenture system
proved inefficient or too costly, slaves were used everywhere to take up the labor slack.[2]

[1] Marcus W. Jernegan, *Laboring and Dependent Classes in Colonial
America* (Chicago: University of Chicago Press, 1931), pp. 45-46.
[2] Ulrich B. Phillips, *American Negro Slavery* (New York: D. Apple-

1

Every colony was a slave colony for the simple reason that some degree of compulsion was needed to
maintain a stable labor force. Slavery was the ultimate
form of compelling labor where workers could not be
obtained in sufficient numbers by any other means. So it
was with New Netherland, where the work of colonization was carried out by the Dutch West India Company,
a private trading company particularly unsuited for the
founding of permanent settlements. Weakly capitalized
from the outset, the company did not have the large
sums necessary for the transportation of settlers, supplies, and agricultural equipment to New Netherland
for the purpose of establishing viable communities.[3]
Moreover, the profits eventually earned by the company's monopoly of Dutch trade with Africa and Curaçao, together with the vast sums gained by raids on
Spanish commerce, were immediately distributed as div-
idends to the shareholders with nothing retained for
long-term investments in colonization. The company
spent only as much on New Netherland as was needed
to maintain the fur trade which yielded immediate and
substantial profits.[4]

The West India Company was willing, even eager,
to encourage the development of New Netherland, but
it was unwilling to invest large sums in colonial experi-
ments. The tightfisted directors hoped that the costs of
colonization could be shifted to individual investors
who might be persuaded to put up the needed capital.
This was the object of the charter of privileges issued in
1629 which offered patroonships to shareholders who

ton & Co., 1918), pp. 98-114; Almon W. Lauber, *Indian Slavery in
Colonial Times* (New York: Columbia University Press, 1913), pp. 105-
117.

[3] Curtis P. Nettels, *The Roots of American Civilization* (New York:
Appleton-Century-Crofts, 1963), pp. 200-201.

[4] *Ibid.*

2

would transport fifty adult settlers to New Netherlar__ within four years. Besides the cost of transportation, the patroons were to provide their tenants with cattle, tools, and buildings. The tenants in turn were to pay the patroon a quitrent and submit to the jurisdiction of his manorial court. Although one patroonship was successfully established by Kiliaen Van Rensselaer, the system failed to attract settlers in sufficient numbers to make the policy work. The prospect of living as feudal dependents of a great landlord had almost no appeal to the ruggedly independent Dutch.[5]

Thus the main obstacle to economic progress from the outset was an acute scarcity of agricultural labor. Although the soil was rich and the climate mild, farming was neglected to such an extent that at times the colony teetered on the brink of failure. The few white servants brought over at company expense deserted agriculture at the first opportunity to seek their fortunes in the fur trade.[6] Every ship which landed in New Netherland had more traders than permanent settlers on board. The Dutch came to New Netherland not to colonize but to earn fortunes with which they hoped to return to Holland within a few years.[7] In effect, they regarded the colony with the same long-term indifference and desire for quick profits that the West India Company pursued as a matter of policy.

Why was it so difficult to attract permanent settlers to New Netherland? The ineptitude of the West India Company as a colonizer is only part of the answer. Even more important was the fact that the Dutch had no rea-

[5] *Ibid.*, pp. 201-2.
[6] E. B. O'Callaghan and Berthold Fernow, eds., *Documents Relative to the Colonial History of the State of New York* (Albany: Weed, Parsons & Co., 1856-57), I, 145. Hereinafter cited as *N.Y. Col. Docs.*
[7] J. Franklin Jameson, ed., *Narratives of New Netherland, 1609-1664* (New York: Charles Scribner's Sons, 1909), p. 89.

son to migrate. Life was too attractive in Holland for them to be drawn permanently from their homes. Times were prosperous there, and they faced none of the political or religious pressures which were so important in stimulating emigration from other countries. Content with conditions in Holland, the Dutch had no reason to embark on a perilous and difficult voyage to a distant land. Adventurers and traders might flock to New Netherland, but the ordinary citizen remained at home. And there he would remain until the primitive stage of colonization had passed and the conditions created which would enable him to improve his lot by migration.[8]

When it became clear that permanent settlers could not be attracted in sufficient numbers, the West India Company decided to create a labor force by transporting slaves to New Netherland. Unable to obtain workers without resort to physical compulsion, and needing labor for its production and development, New Netherland became a slave colony.[9] Beginning in 1626, the company imported parcels of slaves to work on the farms, public buildings, and military works for which free workers were not available.[10] It is doubtful whether New Netherland would have survived without these slaves, for they provided the labor which ultimately transformed the colony from a shaky commercial outpost into a permanent settlement.[11]

8 Charles M. Andrews, *The Colonial Period of American History* (New Haven: Yale University Press, 1934-38), III, 78-80; J. A. Doyle, *The Middle Colonies* (London: Longmans, Green & Co., 1907), IV, 12.
9 *N.Y. Col. Docs.*, I, 246.
10 The total number of slaves in a "parcel"—the principal colonial usage for describing human cargoes—varied from about ten to twenty. See Jernegan, *Laboring and Dependent Classes in Colonial America*, p. 15.
11 E. B. O'Callaghan, ed., *Voyage of the Slavers St. John and Arms of Amsterdam* (Albany: J. Munsell, 1867), p. xiii; I. N. Phelps Stokes,

SLAVERY IN NEW NETHERLAND

Having adopted slavery as an instrument of colonization, the West India Company took measures to encourage the private importation of slaves. In 1648 it
relaxed its commercial monopoly and permitted New
Netherlanders for the first time to trade directly with
Angola.[12] One of the great sources of the African slave
trade, Angola exported large numbers of slaves each
year to all the American colonies. The plan called for
New Netherlanders to send their farm produce to Angola and "to convey Negroes back home to be employed
in the cultivation of their lands."[13] It was expected that
the flow of slaves to New Netherland would promote
agriculture, and that this in turn would increase the
demand for slaves, thereby creating a cycle of prosperity
and agricultural development. To make the trading
privilege as attractive as possible, the company agreed to
remit the duty on New Netherland produce sent to
Angola.[14]

The results, however, were disappointing, for relatively few slaves were imported from Angola. The plan
failed because the principal demand was for Negroes
who had been "seasoned" on the West Indian plantations. Slaves fresh from their African homeland were
difficult to control—"proud and treacherous"—as one
New Netherlander described them.[15] Besides those imported in small parcels, only one cargo of Africans was
landed by a regular slaver, the *Wittespaert,* during the

---

ed., *The Iconography of Manhattan Island* (New York: R. H. Dodd,
1915-28), II, 297; John Yates and Joseph Moulton, *History of the State
of New York* (New York: A. T. Goodrich, 1902), p. 427.
12 E. B. O'Callaghan, ed., *Calendar of Historical Manuscripts in the
Office of the Secretary of State* (Albany: Weed, Parsons & Co., 1866), I,
101-2, 107. Hereinafter cited as *Cal. Hist. MSS.*
13 O'Callaghan, ed., *Voyage of the Slavers,* pp. 101-2.
14 *N.Y. Col. Docs.,* I, 246.
15 A. J. F. Van Laer, ed., *Correspondence of Jeremias Van Rensselaer* (Albany: University of the State of New York, 1932), p. 167.

entire New Netherland period.[16] And the few who were imported generally turned out to be unsatisfactory to most users of labor.[17] Indeed, African slaves did not usually remain in the colony very long. The cargo landed by the *Wittespaert* was snapped up almost immediately by private traders and reshipped to the plantation colonies where the demand for Africans was greater.[18] The diversion of these slaves so enraged the New Netherland directors that a tariff was imposed to prevent the export of slaves in the future.[19]

Most of the slaves transported to New Netherland came from Curaço, the principal slave entrepôt of the Dutch in the West Indies.[20] The island had a rigorous plantation system which annually produced large numbers of seasoned slaves for export. The demand for these slaves was always greater than the supply, for the brutal seasoning process took a frightful toll. Consequently, New Netherland was unable to obtain as many slaves as the directors believed were necessary for the development of the colony. For many years the directors strove to persuade company officials in Curaçao to give New Netherland special consideration in the allotment of export quotas. A priority was finally obtained in 1655 on the assurance of Director General Stuyvesant that slaves allotted to New Netherland would be used "for promoting agriculture and not for lucre."[21]

Besides those imported in the course of trade, many slaves entered the colony through less regular channels.

16 E. B. O'Callaghan, ed., *Laws and Ordinances of New Netherland* (Albany: Weed, Parsons & Co., 1868), p. 191.
17 *N.Y. Col. Docs.*, II, 768.
18 O'Callaghan, ed., *Laws and Ordinances of New Netherland*, p. 191.
19 *Ibid.*
20 O'Callaghan, ed., *Voyage of the Slavers*, pp. 167-69.
21 David T. Valentine, comp., *Manual of the Corporation of the City of New York*, 1842-70 (New York: Francis P. Harper, 1900), (1863), pp. 591-93.

In 1652 the Dutch privateer *De Raaf*, under French letters of marque, seized forty-four Negroes from a Spanish slaver and sold them at New Amsterdam. Since Spain and Holland were then at peace, the owner of the slaves, a Spanish merchant named Ferrara, hurried to New Amsterdam to challenge the legality of the seizure. Although the Spaniard was clearly in the right, the directors refused to give up the slaves. Stuyvesant sought to justify the seizure on the grounds that Spain had long been hostile to New Netherland's commerce. In any case, he insisted that the letters of marque legalized the sale of the slaves as prize property and fully protected the New Netherland buyers. After pressing his claim in the courts for two years without success, Ferrara finally gave up and abandoned the litigation as hopeless.[22]

The steady importation of slaves from all sources stabilized the New Netherland economy. After 1640 agriculture began to expand, new lands were brought under cultivation, and settlers took up farming with a view to remaining permanently. A rapid transformation took place in which the fur trade, previously the economic mainstay, assumed a place of secondary importance to agriculture as farming gained the ascendancy.[23] Slavery helped to prepare the way for this transition by providing the labor which made farming attractive and profitable to the settlers.[24] Slave labor was especially important in the agricultural development of the Hudson Valley, where an acute scarcity of free workers prevailed. So great was the demand for labor in the Hudson

22 *N.Y. Col. Docs.*, II, 24, 31.

23 Edward C. Kirkland, *A History of American Economic Life* (New York: Appleton-Century-Crofts, 1951), pp. 11, 38-39.

24 A. J. F. Van Laer, ed., *The Van Rensselaer Bowier Manuscripts* (Albany: University of the State of New York [New York State Library History Bulletin, No. 7], 1908), pp. 222, 261, 278, hereinafter cited as *Van Rensselaer Bowier MSS.*; Van Laer, ed., *Correspondence of Jeremias Van Rensselaer*, pp. 167-68.

settlements that some planters offered to buy "any suitable blacks available."[25]

Slavery also provided New Netherland with a highly efficient system of labor for public projects. Slaves raised food for the troops garrisoned at New Amsterdam and kept the military works guarding the town in repair.[26] In 1659 slaves were used to build a fort at Oyster Bay to strengthen the company's hold on eastern Long Island.[27] Since these slaves were largely self-sufficient, raising their own food on plots allotted to them by the company, the public labor which they performed accelerated the economic progress of the colony.[28] In effect, they made possible a rapid recapitalization of profits, for the taxes which normally would have been paid by the settlers to support such public works were channeled instead into the productive sector of the economy.

The rapid progress of the economy after 1640 created a demand for slaves that was usually greater than the supply. For over twenty years slave values rose steadily as users of labor drove prices up. Between 1636 and 1646 the price of able-bodied men rose from 100 to 300 guilders—an increase of about 300 per cent over the decade.[29] By 1660 slaves from Angola commanded 450 guilders, and those from Curaçao about 100 guilders more.[30] In 1664—the year of the English occupation—slaves sold in New Amsterdam for as much as 600 guilders.[31] The market of course was set by age, for this de-

25 *Van Rensselaer Bowier MSS.*, p. 642.

26 Berthold Fernow, ed., *Minutes of the Orphanmasters Court of New Amsterdam* (New York: Francis P. Harper, 1907), II, 191.

27 John Cox, ed., *Oyster Bay Town Records* (New York: Tobias A. Wright, 1916-24), II, 697-98.

28 J. H. Innes, *New Amsterdam and Its People* (New York: Charles Scribner's Sons, 1902), p. 9.

29 Van Laer, ed., *Correspondence of Jeremias Van Rensselaer*, p. 167.

30 *Ibid.*, pp. 364-65.

31 Valentine, *Manual* (1863), pp. 593-94.

termined the slave's probable utility and the years over which the buyer could capitalize on his investment. Slaves between sixteen and forty years of age commanded the highest prices, those between twelve and sixteen about two-thirds as much, and those under the age of twelve about one-half as much. There was almost no market for slaves over the age of forty.[32]

Despite the substantial increase in the price of slaves between 1636 and 1664, the West India Company did not profit greatly from the New Netherland slave trade. Because even higher prices prevailed in the plantation colonies, the slaves supplied to New Netherland sold at a discount slightly below the international market.[33] The discount averaged about 10 per cent—the amount of the export duty levied in 1655 to prevent the diversion of slaves to the plantation colonies.[34] Since this discount reduced the size of the slaveholder's investment, the company indirectly subsidized every user of slave labor in the colony. Not only did the company sell slaves at a discount, it also permitted slaveowners to exchange unsatisfactory slaves for company slaves free of charge.[35] The company did not attempt to build up a profitable slave trade but strove instead to promote the economic progress of the colony by keeping slave costs down. The purpose of slavery, as Stuyvesant saw it, was "to promote and advance the population and agriculture of the province."[36]

By pursuing this policy, the company managed to make slavery an economic and efficient system of labor.

[32] *Ibid.*

[33] *Maritime History of New York* (Federal Writers' Project: Philadelphia: Doubleday, Doran & Co., 1937), p. 27.

[34] O'Callaghan, ed., *Laws and Ordinances of New Netherland*, p. 191.

[35] Van Laer, ed., *Correspondence of Jeremias Van Rensselaer*, p. 255.

[36] O'Callaghan, ed., *Voyage of the Slavers*, p. 202.

Despite the sharp increase in slave prices after 1636, it was still possible for entrepreneurs to buy a seasoned slave for about as much as the annual wages of a free worker. In the 1640's free workers, when available for hire, earned about 280 guilders yearly, plus an allowance for food and lodging.[37] During the same period, slaves from the West Indies sold for about 300 guilders and those from Africa for considerably less.[38] Of course, if a slave died or ran away, the slaveholder might lose his entire investment.[39] But even allowing for this and for the other risks of ownership, slavery was an obvious bargain in view of the relatively high price of free labor.

So intense was the competition for slaves that neither the company nor private traders could fill the demand. Nor was the supply available ever evenly distributed. Some—like the English settlers in Westchester and on Long Island—got too few, while others got too many.[40] The New Netherland directors were not above using their official positions in order to get a disproportionate share. Stuyvesant used his connections in Curaçao to obtain over forty slaves for himself, enough to give him the largest slave force in New Netherland.[41] Johan de Decker, one of Stuyvesant's lieutenants, got an allotment of twenty slaves from Curaçao in a single consignment.[42] Besides building up large private hold-

[37] A. J. F. Van Laer, ed., *Early Records of the City and County of Albany and Colony of Rensselaerswyck* (Albany: University of the State of New York [New York State Library Bulletin, Nos. 9, 10, 11], 1915-19), III, 122, 180.

[38] Van Laer, ed., *Correspondence of Jeremias Van Rensselaer*, p. 167.

[39] Berthold Fernow, ed., *Records of New Amsterdam* (New York: The Knickerbocker Press, 1897), I, 362.

[40] *Southampton Town Records* (Sag Harbor: John S. Hunt, 1874-78), II, 207.

[41] Edward T. Corwin, ed., *Ecclesiastical Records of the State of New York* (Albany: James B. Lyon Co., 1901-16), I, 488. Hereinafter cited as *N.Y. Eccles. Recs.*

[42] Innes, *New Amsterdam and Its People*, pp. 42-43.

10

ings, the directors made free use of the company's slaves on their farms at harvest time.[43]

How many slaves New Netherland had at any given time cannot be estimated with much precision. The directors were notoriously lax in compiling statistics of any sort about the colony. No real census was ever taken, and the port records are fragmentary and vague about slave imports. Nevertheless, some inferences can be drawn from the scattered data available. It is known that from 1640 to 1664 slaves were continuously imported and that some of the slave cargoes were quite large. One of these cargoes landed in 1664 by a company slaver, the *Gideon,* consisted of three hundred slaves.[44] Since there were no more than seven thousand persons in the colony at the time, these three hundred slaves accounted for over 4 per cent of the total population. The size of this cargo suggests the existence of an established slave system with a fairly wide market for slaves. Certainly it contrasts sharply with the first cargo of eleven slaves landed in 1626.[45]

The operation of the New Netherland slave system can be described more accurately than its statistical extent. In many ways its operation was unique, for the system was as mild as the realities of chattel slavery probably allowed. There was none of the mutual hatred in New Netherland of the sort that brutalized slave relations in other colonies. The pragmatic Dutch regarded slavery as an economic expedient; they never equated it with social organization or race control. Neither the West India Company nor the settlers endorsed the specious theories of Negro inferiority used in other places

43 David De Vries, *My Third Voyage to America and New Netherland,* in New-York Historical Society, *Collections,* 2d Ser., III (1857), p. 89.
44 Valentine, *Manual* (1863), p. 594.
45 O'Callaghan, ed., *Voyage of the Slavers,* p. xiii.

to justify the system. No attempt was ever made to treat free Negroes differently from the white population. Whatever discrimination existed was religious rather than racial. Jews, for example, were barred from the militia while Negroes were accepted; Jews could not own realty, but Negroes could and did obtain freeholds.[46] Free Negroes were truly free in New Netherland, for there was no racial legislation of any sort to restrict their freedom. They owned white indentured servants, intermarried with whites, and were accepted or rejected by the community on their own merits as individuals.[47] Race as an instrument of social repression simply did not exist in New Netherland.

This freedom from racial self-consciousness gave the New Netherland slave system its distinctive character. Despite their unequal relationship, masters and slaves worked together at the same tasks, lived together in the same houses, and celebrated the Dutch holidays together on terms of easy familiarity. The Dutch were too preoccupied with the everyday problems of economic development to create a rigid slave system with the paraphernalia of a formal slave code. They were quite unconcerned with the institutional organization of slavery. No laws circumscribed the movement of the slaves or regulated the conditions under which they might gain freedom. The casual attitude of the master class together with the ill-defined legal status of the slave tempered the system to such an extent that it resembled in many ways an indenture system.[48]

---

[46] O'Callaghan, ed., *Cal. Hist. MSS.*, I, 162, 368. See Ellis Raesly, *Portrait of New Netherland* (New York: Columbia University Press, 1945), p. 162.

[47] Fernow, ed., *Minutes of the Orphanmasters Court*, II, p. 46; Fernow, *Records of New Amsterdam*, VII, 11.

[48] William L. Stuart, "Negro Slavery in New Jersey and New York," *Americana*, XVI (1922), 353.

SLAVERY IN NEW NETHERLAND

Slavery never became a clearly defined status because the Dutch regarded the system as a mere expedient. What most concerned them was the everyday operation of the system, not its theoretical consistency. Their completely pragmatic approach can be found in the system of "half-freedom" under which slaves were conditionally released from bondage. This system was introduced into New Netherland by the West India Company as a means of rewarding slaves for long or meritorious service. Slaves who obtained half-freedom enjoyed full personal liberty in return for an annual tribute to the company and a promise to perform labor at certain times. A typical grant of half-freedom bound the recipient to pay the company "thirty schepels of maize or wheat and one fat hog, valued at twenty guilders."[49] To clarify their special status, the half-freedmen were given passes which certified them to be "free and at liberty on the same footing as other free people."[50]

Half-freedom benefited the masters as much as the slaves, for in some cases it was a more efficient system of labor than chattel slavery. The largest slaveholder of all, the West India Company, found that it was expensive and inconvenient to maintain large numbers of slaves whose labor was not always needed. Half-freedom provided the company with a corvée which could be used on fortifications and other public works whenever the need arose. Such a system, in effect, enabled slaveowners to be free of the costs and petty nuisances of slaveholding while reserving the right to specific labor and produce from their former bondsmen. In granting half-freedom to three slaves in 1652, Director General Stuyvesant reserved the right to call upon them to perform

49 O'Callaghan, ed., *Laws and Ordinances of New Netherland*, p. 36-37.
50 *Ibid.*

13

minor chores about his household.[51] Such conditions were enforceable, for the half-freedom passes provided that freedmen who defaulted would "forfeit freedom and return back into the said Company's slavery."[52]

That the system also served the convenience of the masters did not impair its popularity among the slaves. Half-freedom was better than no freedom, and there were few slaves who did not prefer it to absolute servitude. Indeed, the principal complaint of the half-free Negroes was that the status could not be passed along to their children. The certificates granted by the company provided that the children of half-free parents were "bound and obligated to serve the Honorable West India Company as slaves."[53] Although the company never attempted to enslave such children, the mere assertion of the right to do so deeply disturbed the half-freedmen. They bombarded the company with petitions for guarantees of freedom for their children.[54] The Dutch settlers supported these appeals with petitions of their own to Holland attacking the company's policy as "contrary to the law of every people."[55] The willingness of whites to join with Negroes in such a matter—in effect, to encourage the growth of a free Negro population—is clear-cut evidence that they did not regard slavery as a system of race control.

In some respects, half-freedom was antithetical to the whole nature of the slave system. It blurred the line between slavery and freedom in a way that raised dangerous and disturbing questions about the slave's actual status. If slavery was only a labor obligation as half-free-

[51] Stokes, ed., *Iconography*, IV, 223.
[52] O'Callaghan, ed., *Laws and Ordinances of New Netherland*, pp. 36-37.
[53] *N.Y. Col. Docs.*, I, 302, 335.
[54] O'Callaghan, ed., *Cal. Hist. MSS.*, I, 269.
[55] *N.Y. Col. Docs.*, I, 343.

dom seemed to imply, then the rights of the slaveowner were clearly less than absolute. The existence of such a half-way status contradicted traditional legal theory that slavery and freedom were mutually incompatible and could not be mixed in any way.[56] The Dutch, however, cared little about tradition and nothing at all about theory. Rather, they developed practical forms of servitude suitable to their everyday needs. Half-freedom took root in New Netherland because it suited the convenience of the settlers and was consistent with the needs of the economy. That the system had theoretical deficiencies bothered the Dutch not at all.

This indifference to legal theory can be traced to the fact that slavery had long been extinct in the countries of Northern Europe at the time New Netherland was founded. The Dutch settlers therefore brought no legal precedents to America which were relevant to slave relations.[57] As in every colony established by North Europeans, slavery in New Netherland was purely the creation of local municipal law.[58] Not that the Dutch were unfamiliar with the general concept of slavery, for international law in the seventeenth century regarded the institution as licit.[59] However, the municipal law of Holland did not, so there were no statutes or judicial precedents to which the settlers could turn for guidance in dealing with slaves.

Nor were the Dutch settlers eager to formulate laws

[56] Thomas R. R. Cobb, *An Inquiry into the Law of Slavery in the United States of America* (Philadelphia: T. Johnson & Co., 1858), pp. 283, 288.

[57] Ulric Huber, *The Jurisprudence of My Time*, tr. Percival Gane (London: Butterworth & Co., Ltd., 1939), I, 21; Dionysius van der Keessel, *Select Theses on the Laws of Holland and Zeeland*, tr. Charles A. Lorenz (London: Edward Stanford, 1855), p. 12.

[58] Cobb, *Inquiry into the Law of Slavery*, pp. 141-42.

[59] John C. Hurd, *The Law of Freedom and Bondage in the United States* (Boston: Little, Brown & Co., 1858), I, 278.

15

of their own which might limit their freedom to deal with slavery pragmatically. Few New Netherlanders, including the magistrates, had any legal training, and most of the settlers had no desire to establish a formal legal system. Thus they did not legislate for slavery but left the regulation of slaves entirely to improvisation. Equity held complete sway, and problems of slave control were dealt with on an individual basis. In the absence of statutes to guide or restrain them, the Dutch magistrates were able to mete out punishments which they thought best fitted the crime or the offender. Although they were sometimes capricious—for instance, sending cabbage-thieves to the stocks with cabbages tied to their heads—they generally dispensed justice sensibly and humanely.[60] Certainly the system never resulted in the judicial barbarism sanctioned by the statute law in other colonies.

That the system was relatively humane can be traced to the fact that slavery in New Netherland required only a minimum display of force to make it effective. The slaves lived quietly, enjoyed good treatment, and could often look forward to eventual freedom as a reward for loyal service. Moreover, slaves seldom committed offenses which affected the white population directly. No slave conspiracies occurred in New Netherland, nor did any serious antagonism exist between masters and slaves. All the evidence available indicates that master-slave relations were good, often marked by mutual affection and respect.[61] Relations between the two groups were informal and generally free of the corrosive hatred which in other colonies helped to create brutal systems of repression.

60 O'Callaghan, ed., *Cal. Hist. MSS.*, I, 112. See Valentine, *Manual* (1849), p. 422.
61 Stuart, *Americana*, XVI, 353.

16

Slaves fared better in New Netherland, but so did their masters, who in turn escaped the sort of terror which oppressed slaveholders elsewhere. During Director General Kieft's Indian war of 1641-1644, arms were issued to Negro slaves who helped in the defense of the Dutch settlements.[62] This willingness to provide the slaves with weapons, though doubtless a measure of desperation in view of the seriousness of the Indian threat, probably would have sealed the doom of the colony if slave relations had not been good. Negro slaves were even used against troublesome elements in the white population. They were used at Rensselaerswyck to enforce the laws of the manor against rebellious tenants. When some of the tenants refused to pay their quitrents, Kiliaen Van Rensselaer ordered the schout of the manor to use slaves "as brute forces against the malevolents."[63]

This spirit of mutual accommodation between masters and slaves enabled the Dutch to maintain discipline with a minimum use of force. When in 1641 six slaves belonging to the West India Company killed a fellow bondsman in a brawl, all the culprits were compelled to draw lots to choose one of their number for execution. No one was actually executed, however, for the magistrates in the end pardoned the unlucky slave who drew the fatal lot on condition of his good behavior in the future.[64]

Such clemency extended even to crimes which affected the white population. In 1647, for example, a female slave convicted of arson was sentenced to death. After the public sentence had been pronounced, the magistrates issued a secret pardon which the sheriff was ordered to withhold until the last moment. Only when

62 *N.Y. Col. Docs.*, I, 415.
63 *Van Rensselaer Bowier MSS.*, p. 642.
64 *Ibid.*, p. 802.

17

all the preparations for the execution had been completed did the sheriff announce the pardon and return the terrified woman to her master.[65] Magistrates loath to impose the death penalty in capital cases often arranged such mock executions.[66] And since offenders never knew whether a pardon would be forthcoming, the practice did not impair the deterrent effect of the sentence. Its only effect was to take some of the death out of the death penalty.

Slaves had the same standing as whites in the courts of New Netherland. They testified in all sorts of cases, not only against one another, but also in cases involving free whites. In 1646 a civil action over the ownership of some wood was decided on the testimony of a single slave, despite the fact that his story had been contradicted by several white witnesses.[67] Although slaves accused of serious crimes were sometimes threatened with torture, such incidents had no relation to race or slavery. Torture was an accepted part of judicial procedure both in Holland and New Netherland.[68] But it had nothing whatever to do with the race or status of the offender. It was used against free whites as well as against Negro slaves to elicit information about serious crimes once the guilt of the accused had been clearly established.[69] No special punishments or police procedures existed for Negroes as a race or for slaves as a class.

The Dutch, however, were not completely color-blind, for they equated race with slavery and regarded

[65] O'Callaghan, ed., *Cal. Hist. MSS.*, I, 259.

[66] *Ibid.*, I, 74, 89. See Raesly, *Portrait of New Netherland*, pp. 152-53.

[67] Fernow, ed., *Records of New Amsterdam*, V, 337-40.

[68] Huber, *The Jurisprudence of My Time*, II, 457-67.

[69] Fernow, ed., *Records of New Amsterdam*, IV, 68. See E. B. O'Callaghan, *History of New Netherland* (New York: D. Appleton & Co., 1855), I, 229 and Valentine, *Manual* (1949), pp. 412, 421.

18

Negritude as prima-facie evidence of slave status. Like the rest of the New Netherland slave system, the equation of race with slavery did not have express legal sanction, yet it was implicit in the organization and operation of the system. Thus free Negroes who could not offer unequivocal proof of their status were always in danger of being enslaved. In 1642 the French privateer *La Garce* arrived in New Netherland with a parcel of Negroes taken from a captured Spanish vessel. Although some of the captives claimed to be free Spanish subjects, they were all sold into slavery without any inquiry into their status under Spanish law. Because of their race they were all presumed to be slaves and the burden was on them to rebut the presumption.[70]

Despite their condition of bondage, the slaves were treated as members of the New Netherland community, not as a caste of inferior aliens fit only for brutalization and repression. The Dutch regarded the slaves as human beings with feelings and ambitions of their own. Evidence of this can be found in the efforts made by the Dutch to convert the slaves to their own Calvinist faith.[71] Clergy and slaveholders alike encouraged the slaves to attend religious services and observe the religious holidays.[72] New Netherlanders regarded proselytization as a civic responsibility, and slaveowners who refused to cooperate were roundly criticized. When the West India Company failed to provide religious instruction for its slaves, the settlers expressed their shock and disapproval in a petition to Holland.[73]

The slaves for their part were willing enough to cooperate with the proselytizers; indeed, they eagerly

70 Valentine, *Manual* (1870), p. 764.
71 *N.Y. Eccles. Recs.*, I, 142, 150.
72 *Ibid.*, I, 489.
73 *N.Y. Col. Docs.*, I, 335.

sought conversion in the belief that it would free them from bondage.[74] They soon discovered, however, that the spiritual solace of religion had no temporal concomitants. Conversion not only failed to bring freedom, but it did not even bring membership in the Dutch church. A convert was not eligible for full membership until he had made a public confession of faith.[75] And this was extremely difficult, for its purpose was to identify the Calvinist elect. The theological knowledge and scriptural expertise needed to accomplish the feat were beyond most whites and almost all the slaves.[76] Moreover, the desire of the slaves for freedom was itself regarded as a bar to church membership. The dominies refused to baptize freedom-conscious slaves on the ground that their motives were "worldly and perverse."[77]

The slaves nevertheless persisted in believing that conversion would bring freedom. The source of this belief is obscure, but many slaves and even some whites held to it well into the eighteenth century. The most likely possibility is that it was based on a garbled version of international law which then regarded the enslavement of heathens as licit.[78] To some this meant that the opposite was true too: that Christians could not be held as slaves and that conversion would free a non-Christian from bondage. This was not true of course, for individual rights—as distinct from national rights—could only be asserted under municipal law, and in no colony did the municipal law recognize a connection between slavery and religion. This, however, did not

74 *N.Y. Eccles. Recs.*, I, 548.
75 *Ibid.*, I, 508.
76 *Ibid.*
77 *Ibid.*, I, 548.
78 Hurd, *Law of Freedom and Bondage*, I, 278.

prevent the confusion between religious and civil status from surviving through most of the colonial period.[79]

Thus slaves remained eager for many years to join the religion of their masters despite every obstacle put in their path. Those unable to qualify for church membership themselves brought their children to the dominies for baptism.[80] But here too they were often disappointed, for the Classis of Amsterdam, the governing body of the church, discouraged the baptism of slave children "as long as their parents are actually heathen."[81] This policy was enforced by most of the New Netherland clergy who refused to baptize slave children "on account of the material and perverted object which the parents have in view, which is nothing else than liberating their children from bodily slavery."[82]

Other slaves resorted to more aggressive action and sought freedom by running away. Escape from New Netherland was greatly facilitated by the refusal of the English colonies to return runaways. The English regarded the Dutch as interlopers on territory belonging to England, and fugitives from New Netherland were harbored as a matter of policy. New Haven and Maryland openly encouraged slaves to defect, and the possibility of gaining asylum in these colonies doubtless influenced many to run away.[83] The Dutch bitterly resented this harassment and took measures to end it. In 1650 Director General Stuyvesant warned the governor of Maryland that asylum was a two-way street, and that

79 *Infra*, pp. 70-73.
80 *N.Y. Eccles. Recs.*, I, 508.
81 *Ibid.*
82 *Ibid.*
83 William H. Siebert, *The Underground Railroad* (New York: Macmillan Co., 1898), p. 291.

unless Maryland desisted he would retaliate by "advertizing free liberty, access and recess to all servants, fugitives, and runaways."[84]

A significant number of white New Netherlanders apparently protected and assisted fugitive slaves. The harboring of fugitives was so widespread by 1640 that the director's council imposed a fine of 50 guilders on anyone who sheltered or fed a runaway. Since the council found it necessary to reiterate the prohibition in 1648 and again in 1658, it is clear that runaways received considerable assistance from whites.[85] It is also clear that the morality of slaveholding, even in the seventeenth century, was far from a closed question. This can only be inferred of course, but it would certainly seem true for those New Netherlanders who put themselves outside the law in order to assist runaways.

The number of slaves who became fugitives cannot be estimated precisely, but the existence of such a problem is in itself evidence of considerable slave discontent. Although the slaves never engaged in organized violence or insurrection, they did not suffer slavery gladly. By embracing the Dutch religion and by fleeing to other colonies, Negro bondsmen conclusively demonstrated their dissatisfaction with slavery. It could not have been otherwise, for slavery by its nature was abhorrent to its victims. In the final analysis, the best that can be said of the New Netherland slave system is that it was free of horror and brutality. This was a good deal by the standards of the times, but for the slaves it was not enough. However humane, the system could never satisfy their inner yearning for freedom and equality.

84 *N.Y. Col. Docs.*, II, 82.
85 O'Callaghan, ed., *Laws and Ordinances of New Netherland*, p. 32.

II. THE NEW YORK
SLAVE TRADE

"AND WHEREAS WE ARE WILLING TO RECOM-
MEND . . . THAT THE SAID PROVINCE MAY
HAVE A CONSTANT AND SUFFICIENT SUPPLY
OF MERCHANTABLE NEGROES AT MODERATE
RATES, IN MONEY OR COMMODITIES, SO YOU
ARE TO TAKE ESPECIAL CARE THAT PAYMENT
BE DULY MADE."
—*Crown Instructions to Governor Cornbury, 1702.*

WITH the establishment of English control
in 1664, slavery entered an era of unprecedented expansion. Under the proprietary rule of the Duke of York
colonial policy was shaped to a large extent by the Royal
African Company, a powerful slave-trading corporation
in which the Duke and other Restoration leaders of
England held a controlling interest.[1] Unlike the Dutch
West India Company, which had used slavery to implement colonial policy, the Royal African Company used
the colony to implement slavery. From the start of the
English occupation the creation of a commercially profitable slave system became a joint project of both government and private interests. The Duke's representatives in New York—governors, councilors, and customs
officials—were instructed to promote the importation
of slaves by every possible means.[2]

[1] Cobb, *Inquiry into the Law of Slavery*, p. 143.
[2] Albert Giesecke, *American Commercial Legislation before 1789*
(Philadelphia: University of Pennsylvania, 1910), p. 34n.

23

The English policy toward slavery became clear as soon as sovereignty passed from the Dutch. The Articles of Capitulation confirmed the legitimacy of Dutch slave titles, and the Laws of 1665 recognized the existence of slavery as a legal institution.[3] Port privileges and warehouse priorities were given to ships carrying African slaves, and measures were adopted to promote the use of slave labor. The Laws of 1665, for example, restricted indentured servitude to those "who willingly sell themselves into bondage."[4] This ended the informal apprentice and indenture system of the Dutch whereby white servants could be bound for indefinite terms. By limiting indentures to stipulated terms, the English made white servants more expensive and difficult to retain. Finally, the prohibition of Indian slavery by Governor Andros in 1679 completed the policy of restricting slavery to bondsmen of African origin.[5]

These measures greatly stimulated the importation of Negro slaves. During the period from 1701 to 1726, 1,570 slaves were imported from the West Indies, and 802 from Africa.[6] The number imported was actually greater, however, since the port records cover only those slaves imported legally. For one year, 1715, the customs officials recorded only 38 slaves from Africa, though at least 40 more were brought in illegally by one smuggler.[7] Likewise, the records show no slaves from Africa for 1726, though one shipper smuggled in at least 150

[3] *Colonial Laws of New York from 1664 to the Revolution* (Albany: James B. Lyon Co., 1894), I, 18; *N.Y. Col. Docs.*, II, 250-53.

[4] *Col. Laws N.Y.*, I, 18.

[5] Valentine, *Manual* (1870), pp. 764-65.

[6] Daniel Parish's Transcripts of Material on Slavery in the Public Records Office in London (1690-1750), p. 33, MS. coll. N.Y. Hist. Soc.

[7] W. Noel Sainsbury *et al.*, eds., *Calendar of State Papers: Colonial Series, America and West Indies* (London: H.M.S.O., 1860-1953), XXVIII (1714-15), 290-91. Hereinafter cited as *Cal. State Papers, Col.*

on a single trip.[8] In any event, the slave population increased much more rapidly than the port records indicate. In 1698 there were 2,170 slaves in the colony; by 1746 the slave population had grown to over 9,000 adults—the largest slave force in any English colony north of Maryland.[9]

The port records, however, are useful in one important respect: they provide a rough indication of the proportion of white immigrants to Negro slaves entering New York. During the period from 1732 to 1754 the following entered the province through New York City: 1,469 Palatines, 362 "other" servants, 170 "passengers," and 1,138 slaves.[10] Thus Negro bondsmen accounted for over 35 per cent of the total immigration passing through the port of New York. But since large numbers of slaves were brought in unrecorded by smugglers, the actual ratio of Negroes to whites entering the province was doubtless much larger.[11]

Although the Royal African Company provided much of the impetus behind the trade, the company failed to make much of a profit from the increased traffic in Negroes. The company was handicapped in its New York operations by a rigid policy geared to a heavy volume of trade. The company insisted on selling its slaves by the cargo at fixed prices regardless of the age, condition, or skills of the slaves involved in a given transaction. While this policy worked fairly well

8 Parish's Transcripts (1720-38), p. 23.

9 Evarts Greene and Virginia Harrington, *American Population before the Federal Census of 1790* (New York: Columbia University Press, 1932), pp. 92, 95-102; E. B. O'Callaghan, ed., *Documentary History of the State of New York* (Albany: vols. I-III, Weed, Parsons & Co., 1849-50; vol. IV, C. Van Benthruysen, 1851), I, 482.

10 Richard B. Morris, *Government and Labor in Early America* (New York: Columbia University Press, 1946), p. 315n.

11 *Infra*, pp. 38-39.

in the plantation colonies where gang labor was used, it was totally unsuited to colonies where only high-quality slaves were in demand. Local dealers refused to buy consignments of undifferentiated slaves for the highly specialized New York market. Unable or unwilling to adapt to local conditions, the company played only a minor role in the New York slave trade. Most of the market went instead to independent traders who imported small parcels of carefully selected slaves.[12]

The slave trade fast became one of the cornerstones of New York's commercial prosperity in the eighteenth century.[13] The demand for slaves—estimated at 1,000 annually by the Board of Trade for New York and North Carolina in 1709—was enormously profitable to the business community.[14] Merchants, traders, and factors fought energetically for a share of the profits, and their efforts were generally well rewarded. The great merchants imported whole cargoes of slaves, while the smaller merchants specialized in the importation of highly skilled slaves for a more limited market.[15] The retail markup was so high—at least 100 per cent—that almost anyone with sufficient capital to import a small parcel of slaves could set up a lucrative business.[16] There were risks of course, but the potential for profits was more than commensurate.

No social stigma attached to slave trading in the

12 George L. Beer, *The Old Colonial System* (Gloucester, Massachusetts: Peter Smith, 1958), I, Ch. 5; Phillips, *American Negro Slavery*, pp. 39-40.
13 John R. Spears, *The American Slave Trade* (New York: Charles Scribner's Sons, 1901), pp. 90-91. See also Cobb, *Inquiry into the Law of Slavery*, I, 154.
14 *Cal. State Papers, Col.* XXIV (1708-9), 209-13.
15 *New York Gazette*, May 17, 1731; *New York Weekly Journal*, February 26, March 12, 19, 1738/39; *New York Weekly Post-Boy*, July 3, 31, August 7, 21, 1749; *New York Mercury*, July 14, 28, 1760.
16 *New York Mercury*, March 30, May 11, 1761; January 10, 31, March 7, June 13, August 25, October 17, 1762; September 10, 1764.

eighteenth century. Some of New York's leading importers, such as Gabriel Ludlow, Philip Livingston, and
Nicholas De Ronde, were men of unimpeachable social
standing.[17] Likewise, many respectable commission
merchants, factors, and general agents engaged in the
trade on a part-time basis without damage to their reputations.[18] Indeed, the entire business community was
deeply involved, for the profits of the importers seeped
down to the insurers, lawyers, clerks, and scriveners
who handled the paper work of the trade. New York
City's vendue houses obtained a considerable share of
their income from slave transactions. Slave auctions
were held weekly, and sometimes daily, at the Merchant's Coffee House, the Fly Market, Proctor's Vendue
House, and the Meal Market. All the commission houses
profited from the trade to some extent, and some—like
the Meal Market—were almost exclusively markets for
the sale or hire of slaves.[19]

The slave trade was by no means confined to repu-
table merchants. Anyone out for a quick profit was
likely to take a hand in the traffic. Captain Kidd, for
example, transported slaves to New York when not
preoccupied with freebooting ventures.[20] Nor did buyers
object to dealing with unsavory types in order to ob-

17 Book of Trade of the Sloop Rhode Island, 1748-1749, MS. coll.
N.Y. Hist. Soc.
18 *New York Weekly Post-Boy*, October 7, 1748; January 16, Febru-
ary 20, March 6, 13, 1748/49; May 1, 1749; June 8, 1752; December 10,
1753; May 20, 1754; March 31, May 19, 1755; September 30, 1756;
July 13, 1772.
19 *New York Weekly Journal*, April 16, May 14, 1739; *New York
Weekly Post-Boy*, March 3, 1747; July 11, 1748; September 25, 1749;
January 8, 1794/50; May 6, 1751; March 20, 1758; March 31, 1760;
April 15, 1762; October 3, 1765; *New York Mercury*, March 22, August
4, 7, 1756; October 30, 1757; March 20, 27, May 22, 1758; July 26,
October 11, 1762; January 24, 1763; August 8, 1763; March 12, April
30, November 19, 1764; October 7, 28, 1765; February 24, July 6, September 7, 1772; January 23, 1775.
20 *Cal. State Papers, Col.*, XVII (1699), 447-48.

27

tain slaves at bargain prices. One parcel of Negroes purchased by Frederick Philipse in 1698 was delivered at Philipse Manor by pirates.[21] Even ordinary sailors did a bit of slave trading, for the masters of vessels bound for Africa often made agreements permitting crew members to bring back slaves.[22] The trade was so lucrative that such agreements were used to induce sailors to sign aboard shorthanded vessels.

Although it increased greatly in volume after 1664, the slave trade retained many of its earlier characteristics under the Dutch. Because of the emphasis on skilled labor, the English traders, like the Dutch, concentrated on West Indian imports.[23] During the first half of the eighteenth century, thousands of slaves were transported to New York from Barbados and Jamaica. Relatively few were imported directly from Africa prior to 1750, except for occasional shipments of African children under the age of thirteen.[24] These youngsters were much more amenable to slavery than their older and less tractable countrymen. So limited was the demand for adult Africans that Governor Cornbury advised traders to consign such slaves to the southern colonies.[25] Indeed, the importation of African slaves was little more than a sideline for traders primarily engaged in the gold and ivory trade.[26]

But the African trade came into its own for a time after 1750, when the revocation of the assiento closed

[21] J. Thomas Scharf, *History of Westchester County* (Philadelphia: L. E. Preston & Co., 1886), I, 30.

[22] Richard B. Morris, ed., *Select Cases of the Mayor's Court of New York City, 1674-1784* (Washington: The American Historical Association, 1935), pp. 701-4.

[23] Parish's Transcripts (1690-1750), p. 30.

[24] Book of Trade of the Sloop Rhode Island, *passim.*

[25] *N.Y. Col. Docs.,* V, 57.

[26] Book of Trade of the Sloop Rhode Island, *passim.*

Spanish markets to English traders.[27] Under the assiento, English traders had enjoyed the privilege of selling slaves to the Spanish colonies; the closing of these markets flooded the English colonies with large numbers of slaves brought from the African slave stations by traders desperately trying to unload their stocks. So many slaves were brought over from Africa between 1750 and 1756 that the wholesale price of slaves in New York declined about 50 per cent.[28] This decline was sufficient to create a market among bargain-minded users of labor. Thus for several years direct imports from Africa increased as traders began to make New York a regular port of call.[29]

The increased importation of Africans intensified competition among importers for a share of the market. Indeed, so intense was the competition that African traders began the practice of selling slaves directly to users of labor. For about a decade the principal wharves of New York City—Schuyler's, Crommelin's, Walton's, and Van Zandt's—served as markets for the sale of African slaves.[30] With prices depressed by the oversupply of slaves, traders had to cut their overhead by dealing with customers directly. Only slaves not salable immediately on the wharves reached the commission merchants and factors.[31] Even at bargain prices, how-

27 Clarence E. Haring, *The Spanish Empire in America* (New York: Oxford University Press, 1947), p. 220.

28 *New York Weekly Post-Boy*, July 14, 1755; December 25, 1756.

29 *New York Mercury*, October 14, 1754; August 18, 1757; July 17, 1758; July 9, 1759; June 16, 30, August 18, 1760; June 29, 1761; October 11, November 15, 1762; June 27, July 11, 1763; July 23, 1770; *New York Weekly Post-Boy*, August 19, 1751; June 1, 1752; May 13, September 16, 1754; July 25, 1757; July 17, 1758; August 6, 1759; June 24, 30, August 21, 1760; October 1, 1761; June 27, 1765; July 23, 1770.

30 *New York Weekly Post-Boy*, July 31, 1749; June 22, 1772; *New York Mercury*, June 16, 30, 1760; July 23, 1770.

31 *New York Mercury*, August 19, 1751; August 18, 1757; July 17,

ever, more slaves were landed than the market could absorb. Hundreds of unsold slaves were confined in makeshift quarters at Perth Amboy where buyers could obtain them at distress prices.[32]

This influx of Africans lasted about twenty years before entering a period of sharp and continuous decline. By 1770 the slave raids had so depopulated the African coast that the supply of slaves began to fall far behind demand. Although the scarcity resulted in higher prices, the traders nevertheless suffered because cargo quotas went unfilled.[33] The cost of slaves at some of the African slave stations increased over 100 per cent between 1760 and 1770.[34] Prices eventually reached levels much too high for New York where the demand remained geared to low prices. After 1770 the market for Africans virtually disappeared in New York.

The scarcity of slaves in West Africa indirectly affected the trade with the West Indies. The island plantation system took such a heavy toll among the bondsmen that continual infusions of manpower were needed. The shortage of slaves in Africa not only increased the cost of replacement, but threatened the plantation system itself. With the African labor reserve fast disappearing, most planters became acutely aware of the need to conserve their working force. Relatively few slaves were thereafter sold for export and then only at prices far too high for the New York market. Thus after 1770 the slave trade between New York and the West Indies also came to a virtual halt.[35]

1758; August 18, 1760; *New York Weekly Post-Boy*, August 6, 1759; June 30, 1760; June 27, 1765.

[32] Ira K. Morris, *Memorial History of Staten Island* (New York: The Winthrop Press, 1900), II, 37.

[33] Miscellaneous Slavery Manuscripts, Box II, R-S, p. 7, MS. coll. N.Y. Hist. Soc.

[34] *Ibid.*, Box I, D, pp. 16, 24; Box II, G, p. 12.

[35] *New York Mercury*, 1770-83.

With the decline of the overseas branch of the trade, the emphasis shifted to local transactions. Indeed, in point of volume, the internal trade was much more significant, for masters for one reason or another were constantly increasing or decreasing their labor force. The entire community had a stake in this trade. Newspapers depended upon it for much of their advertising revenue. To promote the trade, the newspapers provided slaveholders with special services free of charge. Most papers maintained lists of slaves being offered or sought for sale. Others allowed buyers and sellers the free use of their business premises for arranging slave transactions.[36]

Brokers and retail merchants played an important role in arranging slave transactions. Obadiah Wells, a New York City dry goods merchant, began his career as a slave broker by making his shop available to buyers and sellers in the neighborhood. His interest and participation in the trade grew steadily as his commissions increased over the years. Wells eventually extended his operations to all parts of the colony and to other colonies as well.[37] Many other retail merchants acted as slave brokers as a sideline. Few, however, were as active as Wells, and most limited their participation to bringing buyers and sellers together.[38] Their services were nevertheless indispensable in channeling slave labor into productive uses. Without them, neither the trade

[36] *New York Weekly Post-Boy*, May 27, 1751; *New York Mercury*, August 6, 1764.

[37] *New York Weekly Post-Boy*, October 17, 1748; January 16, February 20, March 6, 13, 1748/49; March 12, 1749/50; April 19, 1756; *New York Mercury*, April 19, 1756.

[38] *New York Weekly Post-Boy*, October 7, 1748; May 1, 1749; June 8, 1752; May 20, 1754; March 31, May 19, 1755; September 30, 1756; July 13, 1772; *New York Mercury*, September 18, 1758; October 22, 1759; October 11, 1762; December 19, 1763; June 11, 1770; November 4, 1771.

nor the slave system itself would have functioned very efficiently.

Lawyers and scriveners also played an important role in arranging slave transactions. Their particular specialty was the operation of slave registries which contained detailed information on slaves for sale. The most successful of these registries was operated in New York City by John Knapp, a scrivener. Knapp listed slaves according to age, sex, and occupation for a fee of two shillings.[39] Making regular use of the newspapers to publicize his service, he eventually gained considerable renown as an effective huckster of slaves.[40] Since Knapp's advertising alone was worth the modest registration fee, the registry was used by large numbers of slaveholders. Although Knapp did not negotiate directly for his subscribers, his service was valuable in establishing contact with potential buyers.

From the buyer's standpoint, every slave transaction was strewn with pitfalls. Although some sellers were extremely candid about their slaves, others deliberately concealed defects in order to get better prices.[41] Some disreputable traders mortgaged slaves before passing them on to unwary buyers.[42] Others specialized in purchasing unsound slaves, masking their defects, and reselling them at prices far above their real value.[43] Old slaves, for instance, could be made more vendible by blackening their gray hairs. Moreover, few sellers were likely to reveal hidden character

[39] *New York Weekly Post-Boy,* July 26, 1764.

[40] *New York Mercury,* June 25, July 2, 9, 1764; October 21, 1765; *New York Weekly Post-Boy,* July 18, December 20, 1764; February 21, March 7, August 1, 1765.

[41] *New York Mercury,* December 7, 1761; June 7, 1762; April 16, 1770; May 13, 1771; April 10, 1775; October 21, 1782.

[42] *New York Weekly Journal,* December 31, 1733.

[43] Richard B. Morris, ed., *Select Cases of the Mayor's Court,* pp. 384-87.

defects which might reduce the slave's market value. Buyers who failed to take the personal habits of the slave into account often found themselves burdened with troublesome bondsmen.

Prudent buyers usually reserved the right to cancel the sale if for any reason the slave proved unsatisfactory.[44] The buyer lost nothing if during the trial period the slave died, became ill, or ran away. His only liability to the seller was for losses due to his own negligence.[45] If the sale was absolute, however, the buyer had virtually no redress against the seller.[46] The only legal remedy available was a civil action for deceit, and the buyer could bring such an action only if the seller had made false representations on which he had relied.[47] Both misrepresentation and reliance had to be proved, and the law placed the whole burden of proof squarely on the buyer. Even when a buyer had seemingly proved his case he was by no means certain of winning, for the courts made liberal use of the rule of *caveat emptor*. In one case a New York City court ruled against the buyer of a supposedly healthy slave who died a few hours after the sale.[48]

No stigma attached to a master who sold his slaves, nor did it matter whether he negotiated directly with the buyer or sold to a trader. Moreover, no distinction was drawn between a speculative sale and one that was

[44] Van Laer, ed., *Early Records of Albany and Rensselaerswyck*, III, 493; *New York Weekly Post-Boy*, October 3, 1748; *New York Mercury*, October 11, 1773; August 11, 1777.

[45] *De Fonclear v. Shottenkirk*, 3 Johnson's Reports 170 (New York Supreme Court, 1808).

[46] *Proceedings of the General Court of Assizes*, in New-York Historical Society, *Collections*, XLV (1912), 32. Hereinafter cited as *Proc. Gen. Ct. of Assizes*.

[47] Richard B. Morris, ed., *Select Cases of the Mayor's Court*, pp. 374-75.

[48] *Ibid.*, pp. 368-70, 548-51.

voluntary. Most slaveholders were small farmers and petty artisans who had to buy and sell according to economic need.[49] Slaves were sold to liquidate estates for the benefit of heirs, to satisfy the claims of creditors, and often just to turn a profit on the transaction.[50] There was nothing invidious about turning a profit, for the moral right of an owner to sell his slaves for any reason was universally recognized. The numerous newspaper advertisements of slaves for sale provide convincing evidence that the traffic in slaves was very broadly based.[51]

Such widespread participation made slave transactions relatively immune to most forms of taxation. With so many interests involved, the New York Assembly was reluctant to impose taxes which were almost certain to be widely resented. Despite the urging of several revenue-hungry governors, the lawmakers repeatedly refused to tax slave transactions.[52] The only slave tax ever imposed by the provincial legislature was an emergency levy passed in 1703 to raise revenue for the defense of New York City.[53] Except for minor levies imposed by the towns and counties from time to time, slave property escaped the tax rolls completely.[54] More-

[49] *Infra*, pp. 45-46.
[50] Gerardus Beekman's Day Book, 1752-1757, Beekman Mercantile Papers, MS. coll. N.Y. Hist. Soc.; *Abstracts of Wills on File in the Surrogate's Office*, in New-York Historical Society, *Collections*, XXV-XLI (1892-1908), IX, 103-4, XII, 182-83, hereinafter cited as *Abstracts of Wills; New York Mercury*, September 21, 1772.
[51] *New York Gazette*, 1726-34; *New York Weekly Journal*, 1734-43; *New York Weekly Post-Boy*, 1743-73; *New York Mercury*, 1752-83.
[52] Parish's Transcripts (1729-60), pp. 10, 13; *New York Weekly Post-Boy*, September 27, 1756. See William Smith, *History of the Late Province of New York* (New York: New-York Historical Society, 1829), II, 11-12.
[53] Parish's Transcripts (1695-1713), p. 5.
[54] Charles W. Baird, *History of Rye* (New York: Anson D. H. Randolph & Co., 1871), pp. 182, 393.

over, these local taxes were capitations and therefore did not cover the sale of slaves. This immunity gave slave transactions a privileged status which augmented the profits of the master class. One nonslaveholder on Staten Island complained bitterly against the injustice of requiring his class to bear the same tax burden "as them that has many Negroes."[55]

The external trade, however, was taxed regularly after 1701 when the first tariff was levied on slave imports.[56] Although the tariff was increased over the years, the rates consistently favored slaves from Africa over those from other colonies.[57] One reason the African trade received preferential treatment was that many of the slaves from other colonies—a majority, in the view of Rip Van Dam—posed a threat to the public safety.[58] Since some colonies permitted masters to export slaves convicted of major crimes, including arson and murder, the intercolonial trade involved serious risks for importing colonies like New York.[59] How many of these slaves were channeled into New York cannot be estimated precisely, but the number was probably large. In any event, so many were imported that the Assembly passed a resolution condemning the practice and warning buyers against "refuse Negroes and such malefactors as would have suffered death in the places whence they came had not the avarice of their owners saved them from the public justice."[60]

---

[55] J. J. Clute, *Annals of Staten Island* (New York: Charles Vogt, 1877), p. 69.

[56] *Cal. State Papers, Col.,* XX (1701), 567-68.

[57] *N.Y. Col. Docs.,* V, 178, 185, 293.

[58] Rip Van Dam to the Lords of Trade, November 2, 1731, *N.Y. Col. Docs.,* V, 927-28.

[59] Herbert L. Osgood, *The American Colonies in the Eighteenth Century* (New York: Columbia University Press, 1924), II, 413.

[60] Parish's Transcripts (1713-19), pp. 8-14.

There were additional reasons for favoring the African trade. One was that slaves imported from other colonies had to be paid for in specie, whereas African slaves could be obtained in exchange for local produce. Since the balance of trade with Africa favored New York, the specie yield alone justified preferential treatment.[61] Moreover, such treatment tended to blunt criticism of the tariff in England. Most of the African trade was controlled by Englishmen whose political influence at home had to be considered by the New York Assembly. By giving England's interests favored treatment, the Assembly made it possible for the governors to approve tariffs without actually violating their instructions to promote the African trade.[62]

Both the government and private commercial interests of England were extremely vocal in demanding preferential treatment for the African trade. A slight increase in the African duties in 1728 brought a sharp warning from the Secretary of State against measures which interfered with the African trade.[63] When the same rates were reenacted in 1732, the merchants of Bristol denounced all colonial tariff legislation in Parliament as a blow to England's economy.[64] They raised such a storm in Parliament that only the fear of creating a revenue crisis for the colonial government prevented the Privy Council from disallowing the measure.[65] The Assembly, however, was warned not to extend the objectionable rates beyond the current year. The Board of Trade urged the complete abandonment

[61] Alexander C. Flick, ed., *History of the State of New York* (New York: Columbia University Press, 1933-37), II, 336.
[62] Hurd, *Law of Freedom and Bondage*, I, 280.
[63] Giesecke, *American Commercial Legislation*, p. 32.
[64] *Cal. State Papers, Col.*, XLI (1734-35), 278-79.
[65] W. L. Grant and James Munro, eds., *Acts of the Privy Council: Colonial Series, 1613-1783* (London: Wyman & Sons, Ltd., 1908-12), III, 422-23.

of the African tariff and the substitution of an internal capitation to take up the revenue slack.[66]

The Assembly, however, regarded such interference as invidious to its fiscal prerogatives. To the lawmakers, the issue was nothing less than the fiscal autonomy of the province. Determined to defend its prerogatives, the Assembly reenacted the African duties in 1734 after rejecting a proposal by the Board of Trade that the duties be shifted from the trader to the buyer.[67] This intransigence raised a storm in England, and demands were made in Parliament that the Privy Council disallow the legislation. The Board of Trade, however, urged moderation. Though annoyed at its own rebuff, the Board advised against disallowance until a substitute revenue measure could be passed. Meanwhile, it ordered Governor Cosby to veto any bill extending the African rates beyond 1734.[68]

But Cosby failed to use the veto a year later when the Assembly accepted the challenge and voted to extend the tariff. Torn between his orders from England and the possibility of fiscal reprisals by the Assembly, he bowed to the latter and allowed the bill to pass.[69] The Privy Council, however, took a stronger stand. It disallowed the tariff and warned the Assembly that duties on the African trade would not be tolerated in the future.[70] But this threat could not be carried out, for the Assembly's control of the purse gave it a decisive advantage in any revenue dispute. The Council could not disallow the tariff indefinitely without subjecting English authority in New York to the prospect of fiscal strangulation. Three years later, when tempers

66 *Cal. State Papers, Col.*, XXXIX (1732), 55.
67 *Ibid.*, XLII (1735-36), 30-31.
68 *Ibid.*
69 *N.Y. Col. Docs.*, VI, 32-34, 37-38.
70 *Ibid.*

had cooled somewhat, the Assembly enacted slightly lower rates for the African trade without any objection from the Privy Council.[71]

The furor over the slave tariff harbingered the Assembly's determination to control taxation. The political character of the controversy can be discerned in the Assembly's attitude toward actual enforcement of the tariff. Although all slaves were dutiable, the Assembly voted numerous exemptions under which nonresidents were able to settle in New York with their bondsmen.[72] Such waivers were continually granted, though many nonresidents abused the privilege by importing slaves for sale. The Assembly voted so many exemptions that the port officials complained of the loss of revenue. In 1752 the Collector of New York warned that the numerous exemptions and waivers granted by the Assembly had seriously undermined the revenues of the port.[73]

But the greatest loss of revenue stemmed not from the exemptions but from smuggling. The numerous coves and inlets of Long Island enabled traders to unload all or part of their cargoes before entering port and clearing customs.[74] Many traders chose to land their cargoes in duty-free New Jersey in order to avoid the watchers stationed along the Long Island coast.[75] The customs officials seemed totally unable to bring such evasions under effective control. Nor was the

[71] *Letter Book of John Watts, 1762-1765,* in New-York Historical Society, *Collections,* LXI (1928), 355, hereinafter cited as *John Watts Letter Book.* See W. E. B. Du Bois, *The Suppression of the African Slave Trade to the United States of America, 1638-1870* (New York: Longmans, Green & Co., 1904), p. 19.

[72] Parish's Transcripts (1713-19), pp. 2-5.

[73] *Ibid.,* pp. 6-7.

[74] Andrews, *The Colonial Period of American History,* IV, 83.

[75] Parish's Transcripts (1729-60), pp. 19-20. See *Maritime History of New York,* p. 52.

smuggling limited to a few disreputable traders striving to make an extra profit. Even merchants of otherwise unimpeachable standing, such as John Watts and Gedney Clarke, smuggled slaves with bland disregard for the law.[76] It is impossible to estimate how many were smuggled in each year, but the number was probably large. It was particularly difficult, as Governor Montgomery complained in a report to the Lords of Trade in 1729, to prevent "the importation of Negroes from the neighboring colonies into the remote counties and most obscure places of this province, without entering them or paying the duties, but with an absolute intent to defraud the government."[77]

The prevalence of smuggling reflected the nature of the slave trade, adding only another risk to an enterprise inseparable from risk. Merchants and shipowners who were otherwise upstanding, respectable members of the community repeatedly broke the law to circumvent the tariff. They had no apparent qualms over such illegalities, for some recorded them matter-of-factly as part of the normal course of business.[78] And the risk they incurred was really quite minor, for only one vessel was libeled for slave smuggling in New York during the whole colonial era.[79] With the odds so heavily weighted against detection, it is not surprising that evasions of the slave tariff were so numerous.

76 *John Watts Letter Book*, pp. 31-32.
77 *N.Y. Col. Docs.*, V, 895.
78 *John Watts Letter Book*, pp. 31-32.
79 *Cal. State Papers, Col.*, XXVIII (1714-15), 290-91.

III. THE ECONOMICS OF SLAVERY

"THE PRICE OF LABOR IS NOW BECOME SO HIGH,
AND HENCE THE OWNERS OF SLAVES REAP
SUCH ADVANTAGE, THAT THEY CANNOT REA-
SONABLY COMPLAIN OF A TAX ON THEM."
—*Lieutenant Governor De Lancey, December 7, 1755.*

ALTHOUGH English commercial policy pro-
moted the slave system, the development of the institution in New York was determined by forces indigenous
to the economy. Slavery succeeded mainly because it
served a basic economic need of the province for an adequate supply of labor.[1] After the introduction of slavery, neither the colonial government nor private interests expended much effort attracting free workers or
indentured servants. As a result, most immigrants entered New York on their own initiative and for their
own reasons. Aggressive and independent, they sought
livelihoods as artisans, tradesmen, and farmers. And
since opportunities for self-employment abounded, most
newcomers eventually realized to some extent their
common goal of personal independence.[2] So few entered
the labor market that the dependence of the colony on
slave workers actually increased over the years.[3]

As early as 1699, Governor Bellomont noted in a

---

[1] *Cal. State Papers, Col.,* XVII (1699), 152, 176.

[2] Between 1694 and 1706, 582 artisans representing 80 different trades
were admitted to freemanship in New York City. See Samuel McKee,
Labor in Colonial New York, 1664-1776 (New York: Columbia University Press, 1935), pp. 177-82, and Richard B. Morris, *Government
and Labor in Early America,* p. 156.

[3] One New York City newspaper observed that the labor scarcity

41

report to the Lords of Trade that users of labor "have no other servants in this country but Negroes."[4] During the next fifty years the slave force increased at a faster rate than the white population. Slavery made steady progress in the Long Island townships of Flatbush, Flatlands, Gravesend, New Utrecht, Brookland, and Bushwick. The rapid rate of slave increase in these towns, from 14 per cent of the population in 1698 to 21 per cent in 1738, paralleled a similar expansion of the system throughout the province.[5] On Staten Island, for example, slaves made up 10 per cent of the population in 1698, 17 per cent in 1723, and 21 per cent in 1756.[6] By 1746 Negro slaves accounted for 15 per cent of the total New York population.[7] Although the greatest concen-

---

"partly proceeds from land being easily come at, or vacant, which induces the people to scatter . . . where they content themselves with a scanty living that requires very little labor, and have no ambition to better their condition." *New York Weekly Post-Boy*, June 7, 1764.

[4] *Cal. State Papers, Col.,* XVII (1699), 176.

[5]

	1698		1738	
	White	Slave	White	Slave
Flatbush	405	71	410	129
Flatlands	216	40	195	42
Gravesend	193	17	188	23
New Utrecht	211	48	185	84
Brookland	444	65	547	158
Bushwick	249	52	249	78

Sources: W. A. Rossiter, ed., *A Century of Population Growth in the United States, 1790-1900* (United States Census Bureau: Washington: Government Printing Office, 1909), pp. 11, 181-83; Greene and Harrington, *American Population before 1790*, pp. 93-95; James Riker's Album, I, 187, 191-92, 194-95, II, 138, MS. coll. N.Y. Hist. Soc.

[6] Rossiter, ed., *A Century of Population Growth*, pp. 181-83; Clute, *Annals of Staten Island*, p. 70.

[7]

Year	Percentage Slave	Year	Percentage Slave
1703	11.5	1746	14.8
1723	14.8	1749	14.4
1731	14.3	1756	14.0
1737	14.7	1771	11.8

Source: Greene and Harrington, *American Population before 1790*, pp. 95-102.

tration of slaves was in New York City and the counties closest to the city, the number of slaves increased steadily throughout the province.[8]

This growing slave force, however, failed to keep pace with the labor needs of the colony. With entrepreneurs bidding competitively for the available supply, the price of able-bodied men increased from £16 in 1687 to £40 in 1700 to £60 in 1720.[9] By 1760 the market value of adult male slaves reached £100 while children ten years old sold for £40 and up.[10] The price of slave women was from 20 to 40 per cent lower than that of comparable males. Since they were used mainly for domestic service, slave women returned little in the way of profit to their owners.[11] Moreover, in an urban milieu, their potential for childbearing diminished rather than increased their market value. Although slave births technically increased the owner's capital, the inconvenience to householders with only limited living space more than offset whatever gain eventually accrued.[12]

Despite the heavy demand for all kinds of labor, the market for slaves was highly selective. The most highly prized slaves were the young adults under the age of twenty-five from whom the buyer could expect to ob-

[8] *Infra,* pp. 197-99.
[9] Jacobus Van Cortlandt's Letter Book (1698-1700), p. 61, MS. coll. N.Y. Hist. Soc.; *Papers of the Lloyd Family of the Manor of Queens Village,* in New-York Historical Society, *Collections,* LIX-LX (1926-27), I, 115, hereinafter cited as *Lloyd Papers;* Thomas F. De Voe, *The Market Book* (New York: De Voe, 1862), pp. 245-46.
[10] *Lloyd Papers,* I, 311, II, 584-85; *New York Mercury,* August 21, December 1, 1760; March 30, May 11, 1761; January 10, 31, March 7, June 13, August 25, October 17, 1763; September 10, 1764.
[11] *New York Weekly Post-Boy,* December 19, 1748; January 27, 1752; July 9, 16, October 15, 22, 1753; June 5, July 24, December 11, 1758; May 13, 1771; *New York Mercury,* November 20, 1758; June 7, August 16, 1762; October 29, 1770; October 12, 1772.
[12] One unusually fecund slave woman in Esopus gave birth to twenty-three children by the age of thirty-six. *New York Mercury,* February 15, 1773.

tain many years of service. Some of the largest slave cargoes landed in New York were made up exclusively of slaves under the age of twenty.[13] Also in great demand were slaves who had recovered from a bout with smallpox and thereby acquired immunity to the disease. Advertisements of slaves for sale made it clear that such immunity greatly enhanced the marketability of slaves.[14]

Older slaves, on the other hand, were shunned by most buyers even at bargain prices.[15] As a practical matter, slaves over the age of forty rarely appeared on the market. Rather, they lived out their lives with the masters who owned them during their more productive years. Although one owner in New York City optimistically offered a seventy-year-old slave for sale it is most unlikely that he found any buyers.[16] Likewise, slave women with a reputation for fecundity found few buyers, especially among townspeople whose living space was limited. Infant slaves required attention and care as well as food and living space. They distracted adult slaves from their regular duties and generally disturbed the master's household.[17]

13 *New York Weekly Post-Boy,* July 31, 1749; May 13, 1754; July 25, 1757; August 21, 1760; June 22, 1772; *New York Mercury,* July 9, 1759; June 16, 30, August 18, 1760; January 5, September 20, November 15, 1762; June 27, July 11, 1763; June 24, 1765.

14 *New York Gazette,* October 4, 1731; September 3, 24, 1733; *New York Weekly Journal,* September 23, 1734; April 28, 1735; June 19, 1738; April 16, 1739; March 31, 1740; *New York Weekly Post-Boy,* August 28, 1749; June 15, July 13, August 3, October 23, 30, November 27, 1752; February 12, April 9, 1753; *New York Mercury,* April 18, November 28, 1757; January 23, 30, August 14, October 23, November 6, 1758.

15 *Letters and Papers of Cadwallader Colden, 1711-1775,* in New-York Historical Society, *Collections,* L-LVI, LXVII-LXVIII (1917-23, 1934-35), I, 39. Hereinafter cited as *Colden Papers.*

16 *New York Gazette* (Weyman's), March 3, 1762.

17 A traveler in Albany in the 1750's noted that servile fecundity

Some slaveowners sold their female domestics at the first sign of pregnancy. One master in New York City candidly informed the public that he was selling his female cook "because she breeds too fast for her owner to put up with such inconvenience."[18] Indeed, the mere possibility of sterility increased the market value of most female slaves. One owner offered his slave woman for sale at a premium because "she has been married for several years without having a child."[19] Sterility was so much in demand that owners could sell women well beyond the vendible age for males. One householder in New York City offered to trade a seventeen-year-old girl with many years of potential service for "a middle-aged wench that gets no children."[20]

Moreover, the organization of the slave system itself made fecundity a liability, for the average owner required only one or two men to supplement his own labor in addition to a woman for domestic service. Larger holdings tended to be uneconomic, especially in the towns and on small farms where slave workers required direct supervision. All in all, the slave population was more widely diffused in New York than in any other colony. A census taken in 1755, about one-third complete, reveals the interesting fact that the 2,456 adult slaves counted belonged to 1,137 owners. The ratio of slaves to masters was 133 to 62 in Brooklyn, 88 to 37 on Staten Island, and 81 to 53 at Huntington. The average owner in Rye held only two slaves, and in New Paltz no one owned more than seven. Indeed, only seven

---

had turned some households into "overstocked hives." Anne Grant, *Memoirs of an American Lady* (New York: Dodd, Mead & Co., 1901), I, 266-67.

18 *New York Weekly Post-Boy*, May 17, 1756.
19 *New York Mercury*, April 8, 1776.
20 *New York Gazetteer*, November 16, 1784.

slaveholders in the entire province owned ten or more, while 1,048 owned fewer than five.[21]

Among the larger slaveholders were the great land-owners such as the elder Lewis Morris, who at the time of his death owned a total of sixty-six Negroes.[22] The first Frederick Philipse owned about forty slaves,[23] and Sir William Johnson purchased as many as nineteen slaves at a time.[24] These large landowners were better equipped to accommodate slave children, for they were not as crowded for living space as the petty slaveholders. Philip Ver Planck was able to keep eight children under the age of fifteen in a total slave force of eighteen; Adolph Philipse managed to keep eight in a force of fifteen; and Lewis Morris, who was probably the largest slaveholder in the province, kept a total of twenty-five slave children without any apparent inconvenience.[25]

The larger slaveholders did not maintain slaves for strictly economic reasons. In the eighteenth century a large staff of domestic retainers was regarded as a badge of social distinction. Among many of the rural gentry slavery had as much social significance as it had economic utility.[26] One large landowner in Westchester

[21] Rossiter, ed., *A Century of Population Growth*, pp. 180-85; Charles R. Street, ed., *Huntington Town Records* (Huntington: Long Islander Print, 1887-89), III, 199; Scharf, *History of Westchester County*, II, 667; Clute, *Annals of Staten Island*, p. 70; Baird, *History of Rye*, p. 182; Ralph Le Fevre, *History of New Paltz* (Albany: Fort Orange Press, 1909), pp. 456-57.

[22] Frederic Shonnard and W. W. Spooner, *History of Westchester County* (New York: The New York History Co., 1900), p. 153.

[23] *Ibid.*, p. 194.

[24] MS. 19, Peter Warren Papers, MS. coll. N.Y. Hist. Soc.

[25] *Abstracts of Wills*, VI, 459-62; *New York Weekly Post-Boy*, April 9, 1750; Shonnard and Spooner, *History of Westchester County*, 153.

[26] Martha B. Flint, *Early Long Island* (New York: G. P. Putnam's Sons, 1896), p. 337; Jeptha R. Simms, *History of Schoharie County and Border Wars of New York* (Albany: Munsell & Tanner, 1845), p. 83; Philip H. Smith, *General History of Dutchess County, 1609-1876* (Pawling, New York: Philip H. Smith, 1877), p. 127.

THE ECONOMICS OF SLAVERY

County made it a practice to travel about with three Negro footmen in constant attendance.[27] Members of the urban upper class likewise kept large numbers of retainers. William Smith, for instance, kept a domestic staff of at least twelve slaves to run his household in New York City.[28] Such holdings, however, were atypical, for the bulk of the slave population was owned by numerous petty slaveholders with whom every slave had to pay his way.

This broadly based pattern of ownership in turn promoted the adaptation of slavery to every possible labor need. Slave workers from the start showed proficiency in virtually every field of human endeavor. Those employed in the towns worked as coopers, tailors, bakers, tanners, goldsmiths, naval carpenters, blacksmiths, weavers, bolters, sailmakers, millers, masons, candlemakers, tobacconists, caulkers, carpenters, shoemakers, brushmakers, and glaziers.[29] Many of these skilled workers, particularly the goldsmiths and naval carpenters, matched the best skills possessed by the white artisans. And they were as proficient in the country as in the towns. In the Hudson Valley, estate owners relied heavily on skilled slaves to keep the estates self-suffi-

27 *American Guide Series: Dutchess County* (Federal Writers' Project: Philadelphia: The William Penn Association, 1937), p. 75.

28 Charles B. Todd, *The Story of the City of New York* (New York: G. P. Putnam's Sons, 1888), p. 244.

29 *New York Gazette,* February 28, 1725/26; July 13, 1730; August 17, 1730; March 13, 1732/33; August 27, 1733; *New York Weekly Post-Boy,* December 19, 1748; February 20, 1748/49; May 1, 1749; June 12, 1749; August 21, 1749; August 30, 1756; July 17, 1758; March 26, 1761; September 30, 1762; July 7, 1763; August 25, 1763; February 26, 1767; January 23, 1769; *New York Mercury,* April 12, 1756; August 30, 1756; February 14, 1757; May 22, 1758; August 18, 1760; November 10, 1760; March 23, 1761; September 21, 1761; June 7, 1762; October 24, 1763; January 15, 1770; February 12, 1770; October 8, 1770; July 20, 1772; November 9, 1772; November 1, 1773; December 19, 1774; January 9, 16, 1775; November 10, 1777.

cient.[30] In skill and occupational diversity, slave labor had most of the attributes of free labor. All that really distinguished the free worker from the slave was that the latter derived almost no benefit from his labor.

Urban slaves, both skilled and unskilled, often found themselves locked in bitter competition with free workers. In 1686 the licensed porters of New York City complained that the employment of slaves in the market houses of the town had caused "discouragement and loss to the sworn porters."[31] To protect the porters, the city council passed an ordinance that "no slave be suffered to work . . . as a porter about any goods either imported or exported from or into this city."[32] It was practically impossible, however, to stem the tide of slave competition. By 1691 slaves had invaded the market houses to such an extent that the free porters complained that the competition had "so impoverished them that they could not by their labours get a competency for the maintenance of themselves and families."[33] This was really more a lament than a protest, for the free porters, like the slaves, were inevitably subject to the standards set by the slave system.

Slaves with industrial skills were especially ruinous competitors, for they undercut the economic security and social standing of the white artisans. In 1737, in the face of increasing slave competition, the coopers of New York City complained that "great numbers of Negroes" were invading their trade.[34] In a petition to the Assembly, they protested against "the pernicious custom of breeding slaves to trades whereby the honest and indus-

[30] Grant, *Memoirs*, I, 265-66.
[31] *Minutes of the Common Council of the City of New York, 1675-1776* (New York: Dodd, Mead & Co., 1905), I, 179.
[32] *Ibid.*
[33] *Ibid.*, I, 22.
[34] Parish's Transcripts (1688-1760), p. 1.

trious tradesmen are reduced to poverty for want of employ."[35] Lieutenant Governor Clarke agreed with the coopers and gave strong support to their petition in the Assembly. Urging the need for protective legislation, Clarke condemned slave competition for having "forced many to leave us to seek their living in other countries."[36] The Assembly, however, refused to act, for the wide diffusion of slave property was a powerful argument against attempting to restrict the use of slaves.

The practice of hiring out slaves intensified the effects of slave competition. Masters with bondsmen to spare regularly rented their services to employers in need of cheap labor.[37] The prevalence of hiring broadened the scope of the slave system by enabling many nonslaveholders to draw upon the slave force to meet their labor needs. Advertisements of employers seeking slaves for hire appeared regularly in all the newspapers. Slave hiring was especially common in the towns where artisans usually preferred renting the services of slaves to buying them outright.[38] Though somewhat less common, the hiring system also extended into rural areas where farmers used hired slaves to meet their seasonal labor needs.[39]

Hirers could contract for the services of slaves on

35 Charles Z. Lincoln, ed., *Messages from the Governors* (Albany: James B. Lyon Co., 1909), I, 260.

36 *Ibid.*

37 Abraham Evertse Wendell's Day Book (1760-1793), April 19, 1762, July 9, 1767, April 7, 1768, September 2, 1771, August 28, September 19, 1772, September 8, 1773, MS. coll. N.Y. Hist. Soc.; *Ledger Number I, Chamberlain's Office, Corporation of the City of New York,* in New-York Historical Society, *Collections,* XLII (1909), 3; *Lloyd Papers,* I, 261.

38 *New York Weekly Post-Boy,* March 27, September 4, 1749; February 12, 1749/50; September 9, 16, 1751; April 12, 1764; February 28, 1774; March 6, November 6, 1775; *New York Mercury,* June 2, 1760; September 14, 1778.

39 Wendell's Day Book, April 9, 1762, July 9, 1767, April 7, 1769, September 7, 1771.

almost any basis—for days, months, or years. For slaves hired by the day or week, an oral agreement between the parties usually sufficed. For longer terms, however, a written contract specifying the period of hire, the sort of work to be performed, the wages to be paid, and the hirer's obligations to the slave was customary. Long-term hirers provided the slave with food and shelter while the owner supplied him with clothing.[40] Some owners allowed hirers to deduct the cost of clothing from wages, though such agreements entailed obvious risks. One owner who entered into such an agreement found to his dismay that the clothing allegedly issued by the hirer consumed the entire annual wages earned by the slave.[41]

The hiring system worked mainly because the slaves were sufficiently skilled to compete effectively with all types of free workers. But the system also owed much of its success to the pressing labor needs of non-slaveholders as well as to the profits accruing to the masters. If for some reason an owner did not need all his slaves, he usually preferred hiring them out for a time to selling them. Frequently executors and administrators hired out slaves belonging to estates under probate. It was also commonplace for the heirs, especially widows and dependents of the deceased, to hire out slaves under long-term contracts and thereby free themselves of the burden of supervision.[42]

Although convenient to the slaveholder in some respects, the transfer of supervisory responsibility had certain built-in disadvantages. For one thing, the owner had difficulty protecting his investment in the slave. If,

[40] Van Laer, ed., *Early Records of Albany and Rensselaerswyck*, III, 546.
[41] *Lloyd Papers*, I, 261, 277.
[42] *Abstracts of Wills*, X, 63-64, 271-72.

for example, the hirer did not provide the slave with adequate food, if he overworked him or used him for dangerous work which resulted in injury or death, the owner suffered to some extent a loss of capital.[43] Losses caused by the hirer's negligence were legally compensable if negligence could be proved, but some losses by their nature were not even actionable. Hiring, for example, undermined morale, for it impressed upon the slaves the exploitative nature of the master-slave relationship. As slaves served under successive hirers, bonds of personal loyalty weakened and discipline inevitably became more difficult to maintain.[44]

The profit to the owner, however, apparently outweighed every other consideration, for hiring proliferated to an extent probably unequaled in any other colony. Small farmers unable to afford to buy slaves outright or to employ them profitably throughout the entire year hired them instead to meet their seasonal labor needs.[45] But the greatest demand came from urban householders and artisans. The average householder preferred to hire rather than purchase domestic servants. Advertisements for cooks, coachmen, gardeners, and laundresses filled New York City newspapers in the eighteenth century. Likewise, artisans whose labor needs fluctuated from time to time advertised for the services of skilled slaves.[46]

For over a century the demand for hired slaves

43 See *New York Mercury*, April 12, 1756.
44 *Lloyd Papers*, I, 256.
45 Wendell's Day Book, April 9, 1762, July 9, 1767, April 7, 1769, September 7, 1771.
46 *New York Weekly Post-Boy*, March 27, 1749; September 4, 1749; February 12, 1749/50; September 9, 16, 1751; April 12, 1764; February 28, 1774; March 6, November 6, 1775; *New York Mercury*, June 2, 1760, *et seq.*

closely approximated the number available for hire.[47] After 1770, however, the demand far exceeded the supply. That an imbalance should arise was inevitable, for the decline of imports and the rise of manumissions in the late eighteenth century made slaves increasingly scarce. And the American Revolution after 1775 aggravated the scarcity by cutting off the overseas slave trade completely. Moreover, the war itself encouraged the use of hired slaves as a desirable alternative to purchasing bondsmen. Military operations so disrupted slave relations in New York that the outright purchase of slaves became a hazardous form of investment.[48] Thus the demand for hired slaves increased at the very time that the supply of slaves available for hire was declining.

Hiring rates varied in different parts of the province according to local conditions, the needs of the employer, and the skills of the slaves. Skilled slaves of course commanded higher wages than the unskilled, and the earning power of women fell considerably below that of men. As slave values rose in the eighteenth century, the wage rate also increased. Ordinary laborers who earned £5 yearly in 1695 commanded £20 by 1725.[49] By 1760 adult slaves rented for £60 per year or more depending upon the slave's skill and training.[50] In the 1770's wages reached unprecedented heights as employers bid for the declining number of slaves available for hire. An able-bodied man could not be hired

<hr>

[47] The number of "wanted for hire" advertisements in the newspapers roughly equaled the "offered for hire" advertisements prior to 1770. See *New York Gazette* (1726-34), *New York Weekly Journal* (1734-43), Weyman's *New York Gazette* (1759-67), *New York Weekly Post-Boy* (1743-73), *New York Mercury* (1752-83).

[48] *Infra*, pp. 154-57.

[49] *Lloyd Papers*, I, 147, 161, 258. See Richard B. Morris, *Government and Labor in Early America*, pp. 237, 266.

[50] Livingston Family Account Book (1760-1787), p. 3, MS. coll. N.Y. Hist. Soc.

for less than £100 annually and even children earned up to £60 per year.[51] Although inflation certainly helped to drive up the hiring rate, slave wages—like slave prices—rose more sharply than the general price level.[52]

Slaves hired by the day earned more than those hired at monthly or yearly rates. But the net return to the owner was not necessarily greater, for slaves hired out by the day usually lived at home. Not only did the owner have to maintain the slave out of the wages received, but he had to allow for frequent periods of idleness during which he received no income at all. The daily wages of a female domestic at New York City in 1750 were two shillings as against sixteen shillings on a monthly basis.[53] Likewise, slave sailors could be hired for 2.6 shillings by the day or for 60 shillings per month.[54] Regardless of the period of service, however, the type of work to be performed was the principal factor in determining the hiring rate. One owner in Albany hired his slave out at a daily rate of 8 shillings for plowing, 5 shillings for mowing wheat, and 4 shillings for cutting wood.[55]

These rates were profitable to hirers and owners alike. Since white workers commanded a daily wage of about 5.6 shillings by 1760, slave labor cost employers only about half as much as the going rate of free labor.[56]

51 *New York Mercury,* July 10, 1780; April 21, 1783.

52 Arthur E. Cole, *Wholesale Commodity Prices in the United States, 1700-1861* (Cambridge: Harvard University Press, 1939), pp. 30, 52-53. See also Herman M. Stoker, "Wholesale Prices at New York City, 1720-1800," *Cornell University Agricultural Experiment Station Memoirs,* No. 142 (Ithaca, 1932), pp. 201-2.

53 Thomas Witter's Account Book (1747-1768), January, July, 1747; May, 1750, MS. coll. N.Y. Hist. Soc.

54 *Ibid.,* January 25, 1753; Witter's Wage Receipts (1767), MS. coll. N.Y. Hist. Soc.

55 Abraham Evertse Wendell's Account Book (1760-1793), August 1, 1763, August 1, 1764, June 3, 1765, MS. coll. N.Y. Hist. Soc.; Wendell's Day Book, May 13, 1763.

56 John Pryor's Account Book (1762-1767), April 10, 1762, MS. coll. N.Y. Hist. Soc.

And the rates were sufficient to provide slaveowners with an excellent return on their investment. Although wages fluctuated with changing economic conditions, slaves consistently returned from 10 to 30 per cent annually on their market value. Slaves valued at £40 in 1695 earned £5 per year plus maintenance—a net return of about 12 per cent on the owner's investment.[57] And the yield increased considerably in the eighteenth century. Slaves appraised at £70 in 1725 earned £20 per year —a net return of 29 per cent.[58] When wages and prices soared during the Revolution, slaves could be hired out by the year at from 40 to 60 per cent of market value.[59] These rates of course were abnormally high and must be discounted accordingly; nevertheless, even the rates prevailing before the war sufficed to make slaves a highly profitable form of investment.

The profits of course did not accrue evenly to all owners of slaves. Some profited more than others, and for some the slave system was less economic than a system of free labor. Free workers could be hired or fired as needed, but slaves had to be supported whether they were needed or not. Employers had no obligation to free workers beyond the term of their employment. They could cast them adrift to become a public charge when they grew too old or infirm for useful labor. Slaveholders, however, could not dispose of their workers at will, for the law obligated them to support their slaves.[60] Many slaveowners found that the expense of providing infirm slaves with medical care cut deeply into the profits of the system.[61]

[57] Jacobus Van Cortlandt's Letter Book, p. 61.
[58] Parish's Transcripts (1720-38), p. 5; *Lloyd Papers*, I, 307.
[59] *New York Mercury*, July 10, 1780; April 21, 1783.
[60] *Infra*, pp. 141-42.
[61] Philip Evertse Wendell's Day Book (1754-1760), p. 30, MS. coll. N.Y. Hist. Soc.; *Lloyd Papers*, I, 309-10, 341, II, 719.

How much it cost to maintain a slave cannot be determined precisely, for a slave's upkeep was usually included in the general costs of the slave owner's household. If the owner maintained a high standard of living, his slaves also lived well; if the standard was low, then the slaves did not live as well. Most slaves were well clothed, for it seems to have been the practice to buy new clothing for slaves rather than to pass along old clothes discarded by members of the slaveholder's family. Charles Nicoll did a thriving retail business in New York City providing ready-made clothing for slaves.[62] One slaveholder in Albany purchased shoes for his slaves from his own bootmaker.[63] While one owner might outfit his slaves with cheap, ready-made clothing, another might provide his slaves with expensive imported attire.[64] Ultimately what it cost to maintain a slave depended on the generosity and personal whims of the individual master.

The costs of maintenance, however, probably weighed most heavily on rural owners whose labor needs were limited by the relatively short growing season.[65] Farmers sometimes found that the cost of maintaining slaves during the idle winter months consumed the entire year's profits.[66] Likewise many urban owners found the system onerous and expensive. The large amounts of capital that had to be tied up in labor increased the

[62] Charles Nicoll's Account Book (1753-1759), January 27, October 24, 1756, October 2, 1760, March 21, 1761; Ledger (1759-1765), pp. 4, 9, 11, 13-16, 33, MS. coll. N.Y. Hist. Soc.

[63] Abraham Wendell's Ledger (1740-1754), p. 3, MS. coll. N.Y. Hist. Soc.

[64] Thomas Witter's Account Book (1747-1758), passim; Charles Nicoll's Ledger (1759-1765), p. 11.

[65] Colden Papers, II, 30-34.

[66] Henry A. Stoutenburg, ed., Documentary History of the Dutch Congregation of Oyster Bay (New York: The Knickerbocker Press, 1902-7), VII-X, 752. See also Ira K. Morris, Memorial History of Staten Island, II, 36.

business costs of the small entrepreneur. And there was always a chance of losing all or a substantial part of the investment if the slave became ill or ran away. Artisans with limited labor needs often purchased slaves in common in order to reduce the cost of maintenance along with the risk to capital.[67]

Every slaveholder had to bear capital costs in the form of interest and depreciation. Since the interest rate in the eighteenth century ranged from 7 to 9 per cent on prime investments, the return on capital invested in slaves had to be discounted accordingly. And since age reduced a slave's market value, the capital invested in the slave eroded continually. One slave purchased for £70 in 1754 at the age of thirty brought only £50 when sold twelve years later.[68] Thus, despite a general increase in slave prices over the years, the owner's investment depreciated at a rate of about 2.5 per cent per year. Between interest and depreciation, the cost to this owner's capital averaged about 10 per cent per year.

Although fixed costs, interest, and depreciation cut deeply into profits, slavery was nevertheless an efficient and profitable system of labor. Certainly it promoted the rapid progress of the provincial economy. Although a system of free labor offered certain theoretical advantages, there was really no alternative to the slave system. Slaves were in fact the only workers available in sufficient numbers, and employers therefore had to make the most of the system notwithstanding its incidental disadvantages.[69] Some made their adjustment by hiring or purchasing slaves in common and thereby avoided the burdens of outright ownership. Hirers of course could

67 Misc. MSS., Slavery, Box I, Bill of Sale (March 16, 1771); *Abstracts of Wills*, V, 134; VI, 94-95; VII, 28-30; XI, 135; XIII, 111-12.

68 *Huntington Town Records*, II, 418-20.

69 *Cal. State Papers, Col.*, XVII (1699), 152, 176.

have used free labor if it had been more profitable to do so. That they relied so heavily on slaves instead is convincing evidence of the efficiency of the slave system.

The composition of the master class provides the best evidence of the profitability of slavery. The overwhelming majority of the slaveholders were small entrepreneurs who lacked the means to maintain a slave system for noneconomic reasons. The slave prices and hiring rates which they paid were carefully calculated to produce a profit. Certainly there was no doubt among contemporaries such as Lieutenant Governor De Lancey as to the profitability of slavery. In a message to the Assembly in 1755, De Lancey noted that "the owners of slaves reap such advantages that they cannot reasonably complain of a tax on them."[70] But that it paid at all was due to the Negro's ability to master the numerous skills needed to make it profitable. In the final analysis, slavery worked in New York only because the Negro bondsman was as proficient and productive as his white competitor.

70 Lincoln, ed., *Messages from the Governors*, I, 618.

IV. THE NEGRO
UNDER SLAVERY

"ANOTHER INSTANCE IN WHICH I CONCEIVE I
AND MY FELLOW SERVANTS ARE MORE HARDLY
DEALT WITH THAN THE NEGROES, IS THAT
THEY UNIVERSALLY ALMOST HAVE ONE DAY IN
SEVEN WHETHER TO REST OR TO GO TO
CHURCH OR SEE THEIR COUNTRY FOLKS—BUT
WE ARE COMMONLY COMPELLED TO WORK AS
HARD EVERY SUNDAY."
—*Richard Cain to William Kempe, October 23, 1754.*

SLAVE relations after the English occupation were not as good as under the Dutch, for the
rapid progress of the colony and the growth of the slave
population created regulatory problems which were unknown in New Netherland. Nevertheless, relations were
generally good by the standards of the times, and the
government took measures to protect the slaves as well
as regulate them. A law enacted in 1686 made the willful killing of a slave a capital offense.[1] And in 1709
Governor Hunter was instructed by England to see to
it that private slave discipline was not unduly severe
and that the physical needs of slaves were not neglected
by masters.[2] Owners were forbidden to allow their slaves
to beg under penalty of a fine of £10 for each offense.[3]
Moreover, slaves were encouraged to report abusive

1 *N.Y. Col. Docs.*, III, 374.
2 *Ibid.*, V, 138.
3 Flick, ed., *History of the State of New York*, II, 300.

treatment to the provincial council.[4] All in all, the English authorities strove to keep the slave system as humane as possible.

The rationale of slavery of course was race, but the test of race really applied only to the first slaves. With the passage of time and the growth of a racially mixed population, the simple racial test became obsolete from a legal standpoint. By the end of the seventeenth century slave status no longer depended upon Negro blood but upon slave blood on the maternal side. The offspring of a male slave and a free woman was free, and the offspring of a free man and a slave woman was a slave.[5] Thus slavery was not confined exclusively to Negroes but included anyone with slave blood on the maternal side. The slightest admixture of slave blood was legally sufficient to subject a person to slavery regardless of complexion or physical appearance.[6] Persons of predominantly Negro ancestry were often free, whereas persons visibly white were slaves. By the eighteenth century the latter had become quite numerous. Advertisements for fugitive slaves make it clear that some runaways gained freedom simply by passing over into the white population.[7]

In cases where the status of racially mixed persons was in doubt, the courts had to decide who were to be treated as Negroes and who were to be treated as whites.

---

[4] O'Callaghan, ed., *Cal. Hist. MSS.*, II, 371.

[5] Cobb, *Inquiry into the Law of Slavery*, p. 67.

[6] A statute of 1706 provided that "all and every Negro, Mulatto, and mestee bastard child and children, who is, are, and shall be born of any Negro, Indian, or mestee, shall follow the state and condition of the mother." *Col. Laws N.Y.*, I, 597-98.

[7] *New York Weekly Post-Boy*, August 27, 1759; June 18, 1761; March 18, 1771; *New York Mercury*, July 17, 1758; June 15, 1761; May 10, August 30, 1762; October 10, 1763; November 19, 1764; July 20, 1772; October 12, 1776.

The resolution of this question could be vitally important, for Negroes as a class were presumed to be slaves. A Negro claimed as a slave had the burden of rebutting the claim, whereas a white had no burden of proof because the law presumed him to be free. The test was physical appearance, and persons visibly white or Negro were treated as such for the purpose of allocating the burden of proof.[8] When Thomas Thatcher, a resident of New York City, claimed a predominantly white mulatto as a slave in 1677, the court gave him eight days to prove his claim; in the meantime the mulatto was presumed to be free.[9] Although the visibility test could and did result in injustice, it was the only practical test available for a slave system based upon race. Moreover, it was not conclusive as to the ultimate question of status, for in every case the putative slave had the right of rebuttal.

Although the formal structure of slavery was not unusual, its everyday operation was in some ways unique. For one thing, the efficiency of the system required a high degree of collaboration between masters and slaves. Since a large proportion of the bondsmen were highly skilled workers who could not be managed efficiently through coercion alone, concessions had to be made in order to obtain their cooperation. Masters who owned such slaves were usually willing to close their eyes to minor breaches of discipline and even to pay bribes in the form of clothing, liquor, and small sums of money in order to obtain loyal service. There were few concessions within reason that could not be extorted from the masters. The most highly skilled slaves bargained for manumission and were even able

8 Cobb, *Inquiry into the Law of Slavery*, p. 67.
9 O'Callaghan, ed., *Cal. Hist. MSS.*, II, 56.

to prevent unwanted sales by indicating their reluctance to work for a prospective buyer.[10] The value of skilled slaves of course depended largely on their willingness to work. Threats which might be sufficient to compel physical exertion could not on the other hand guarantee the quality of the performance. Such was their bargaining power that skilled slaves were known to break up auctions merely by announcing their unwillingness to work for any of the bidders.[11]

The concessions won by the skilled slaves set precedents which affected the entire slave system. Not every slave of course was able to bargain effectively for freedom; only skilled slaves could do so, for without occupational skill a slave had nothing with which to bargain. The privileges enjoyed by the skilled bondsmen nevertheless brought a spirit of give and take to slave relations in general that made the system more humane in everyday operation. Slaves usually received adequate food, clothing, medical care, and time off for rest and relaxation.[12] With one day off in every seven, they often had more leisure time than white indentured servants, who were usually required to work a full seven-day week.[13] Nor is there any evidence that the mortality rate was higher among Negroes than among whites. Indeed,

[10] Register of Manumissions, pp. 65-66, 73, MS. coll. Museum of the City of New York; *John Watts Letter Book*, p. 151; *Huntington Town Records*, III, 142; *New York Weekly Post-Boy*, March 23, 1746/47; March 30, 1747; August 30, 1756; January 8, 1758; September 1, 1763; *New York Mercury*, September 5, 1763; May 27, 1765; February 26, June 1, 1772; January 18, April 26, 1773; March 4, November 10, 1777.
[11] Schermerhorn to Clinton, January 13, 1788, in Beekman Papers, Box 32, MS. coll. N.Y. Hist. Soc.
[12] Philip Evertse Wendell's Day Book, p. 30; *Lloyd Papers*, I, 341, 309-10, II, 719.
[13] Richard Cain to William Kempe, October 23, 1754, in John Tabor Kempe Papers, Box 4, Folio A-C, MS. coll. N.Y. Hist. Soc. See Richard B. Morris, *Government and Labor in Early America*, pp. 478-79.

against the most dreaded epidemic disease of colonial times, smallpox, Negroes often fared better than whites.[14] Perhaps the most unusual privilege enjoyed by the slaves was the privilege of owning private property. Slaves were allowed to accumulate property for their own purposes without fear that it might be taken from them by the masters. Although the privilege had no legal standing, in practice it was universally respected and protected. Evidence of this can be found in the numerous legacies given to slaves in the eighteenth century.[15] These legacies, made by persons with firsthand knowledge of slavery, could easily have been conditioned on the slave's right of enjoyment if there had been the slightest chance that the proceeds might be taken by the masters. The fact that testators did not make use of this obvious protective device is convincing evidence that they did not regard it as necessary. The property privilege was in fact so well established that the slaves themselves often drew up wills leaving their possessions to friends and relatives.[16]

What use they made of property that came their way depended on the character and outlook of the individual slave. Some bondsmen sedulously saved every penny in order to buy their freedom.[17] Others, however, sought immediate satisfactions and wasted whatever came into their possession on frivolous luxuries. A mania for fine clothing, for example, caused many slaves

[14] During the New York City epidemic of 1730, only 71 of the 509 persons who died were Negroes. Although Negroes constituted at least 20 per cent of the population, their mortality rate was only 12 per cent. John Duffy, *Epidemics in Colonial America* (Baton Rouge: Louisiana State University, 1953), pp. 78-80.

[15] *Abstracts of Wills*, VII, 129, 380-81, 407; IX, 72; XII, 155-57; XIV, 1-3; XV, 112-13, 127-28.

[16] Register of Manumissions, p. 87.

[17] *Jamaica Town Records* (New York: Long Island Historical Society, 1914), III, 346-47, 349-55; *Abstracts of Wills*, XV, 114-16.

63

to squander the wages earned during their free time on the latest fashions. Tailors and bootmakers in New York City did a profitable business outfitting slaves with fancy shoes and fine clothing.[18] The desire to own such apparel was responsible for much petty crime, for slaves unable or unwilling to hire their free time often resorted to theft and burglary.[19] The sartorial mania inspired so much petty theft that some masters tried to protect themselves against pilferage by rewarding loyal slaves with special clothing.[20]

The exaggerated importance given to fine clothing was a natural reaction of the slaves to the general deprivations inherent in bondage. Slaves obtained in expensive attire an illusion of importance that their real condition denied them. Classed as property, it was difficult if not impossible for them to grasp normal social values. Marital and family ties, for example, meant little or nothing to most of the slaves. The average slave lived for satisfactions as ephemeral as the fine clothing which he yearned to own. Perhaps the greatest tragedy of slavery was the way it distorted the outlook of the Negro bondsman and imposed on him a mean and frivolous view of himself. In place of the stabilizing ties of family life, slavery conditioned the Negro to values which were petty and inferior by the standards of the whites.[21]

18 Charles Nicoll's Account Book (1753-1758), January 27, October 24, 1756; October 2, 1760; March 21, 1761; Ledger (1759-1765), pp. 4, 9, 11, 13-16, 33.

19 Joel Munsell, ed., *Collections on the History of Albany* (Albany: J. Munsell, 1865), II, 382-83; *New York Weekly Post-Boy*, April 15, 1762.

20 Hendrick Denker's Account Book (1747-1758), *passim*, MS. coll. N.Y. Hist. Soc.; Charles Nicoll's Ledger (1759-1765), p. 11; *Lloyd Papers*, II, 725.

21 This frivolous attitude toward life in general and toward themselves in particular tends to support Stanley M. Elkins' thesis that slavery "infantilized" the values of many bondsmen. Elkins, *Slavery* (New York: Grosset & Dunlap, 1963), pp. 103-15.

Not that every master was indifferent to the family ties of his slaves, for many of them were obviously troubled by the destructive effect of slavery on the slave family. Some tried to improve conditions by solemnizing slave marriages with civil or religious ceremonies calculated to upgrade the significance of the marital relationship.[22] Curfew regulations were frequently relaxed to permit married slaves to visit their spouses in the evening.[23] Men were often released from their regular duties to spend extra time with their wives and children.[24] It was not unusual, either, for a master to refuse to sell married slaves unless the buyer promised to keep the spouses together.[25]

But for most of the slaves family attachments were casual and impermanent. The slave system was simply not structured to support slave families and no amount of good will could surmount this fact or mitigate its effects. Slave families that were somehow kept together inevitably burdened slaveholders with costly and unmanageable numbers of slave children.[26] Another difficulty was that the typical slave family was divided among several owners. Although one of the owners might be willing, even eager, to protect family ties, he was powerless to do so without cooperation from the others. Since it was economically unfeasible for slaveholders as a class to subordinate their buying and selling to the stability

22 Grant, *Memoirs*, I, 265-67.

23 William S. Pelletreau, ed., *Records of the Town of Smithtown* (Huntington: Long Islander Print, 1898), p. 170.

24 David Humphreys, *An Account of the Endeavours Used by the Society for the Propagation of the Gospel in Foreign Parts to Instruct the Negro Slaves in New York* (London, 1730), p. 7.

25 *New York Weekly Post-Boy*, March 23, 1746/47; March 21, November 28, 1765; *New York Mercury*, March 5, November 19, 1770; February 8, 1779; *Abstracts of Wills*, V, 99-100; VI, 97-98; XII, 374-75.

26 *New York Weekly Post-Boy*, April 9, 1750; *Abstracts of Wills*, VI, 459-62; Shonnard and Spooner, *History of Westchester County*, p. 153.

of the slave family, it was inevitable that families should disintegrate.

Even when slave families were not physically disrupted, the absence of normal economic conditions weakened their stability. The men could not support their families, for they spent most of their time at tasks which benefited the masters. Most of them in fact had no desire or motivation to support their wives and children, for they understood this to be the responsibility of the masters. Whatever economic significance the slave family had involved the sort of responsibilities which fell entirely to the women. Men neither were the head of the family, nor did they have anything to do with the raising of children. It was the mother who provided the children with the essentials of life and with a symbol of authority and protection.[27] Indeed, newspaper advertisements of slaves for sale make it clear that women with dependent children were looked upon as complete family units without the father.[28]

Such conditions created a bad climate of sexual morality. Most slaves regarded monogamy as an aberration when they regarded it at all, for spouses who might be separated at any time by sale were not likely to develop deep emotional loyalties to one another.[29] And the example of the whites was certainly not a source of moral edification. Slavery bound whites and Negroes in a relationship debasing to the standards of both races. For one thing, the defenseless condition of the slave woman was a constant invitation to sexual exploitation.

27 This was typical of Negro family life everywhere under the American slave system. See Kenneth Stampp, *The Peculiar Institution* (New York: Alfred A. Knopf, 1956), pp. 343-44.

28 *New York Weekly Post-Boy* (1743-73); *New York Mercury* (1752-83).

29 *Revolutionary and Miscellaneous Papers*, in New-York Historical Society, *Collections*, XI-XIII (1878-80), III, 355. Hereinafter cited as *Rev. and Misc. Papers*.

How much of this took place cannot be estimated with much precision, for disreputable practices of this sort were carefully kept out of sight. But evidence that such contacts were common can be found in the emergence of a mixed race with various degrees of white and Negro blood. By the middle of the eighteenth century large numbers of mulattoes could be found in all parts of the province.[30]

How the slaveholders regarded their mixed progeny is also hard to determine, for such relationships were rarely acknowledged openly. There is nevertheless considerable indirect evidence that some among the master class treated their mulatto children with affection and compassion. The best evidence of this can be found in testamentary emancipations which hint at bonds of affection much stronger than usual master-slave relationship. Some of the masters who freed mulatto children by will set up generous trust funds to provide for their education and future well-being.[31] One master in Westchester County instructed his executors "to take charge of my little Negroes and bring them up to a good business."[32] One in New York City left his entire estate to three mulatto children in his household.[33] The generosity and affection evidenced by some of the bequests strongly suggest that the beneficiaries were offspring of the masters.

But the most important point of contact between the races after the English occupation was not blood but religion. Racial intermixture was always tainted with

30 Grant, *Memoirs*, I, 85-87.

31 *Abstracts of Wills*, V, 61-62, 113-14, 165-66; VI, 165-66, 275, 417; VII, 34-36, 147-48, 266, 346-47; VIII, 32, 243-45; IX, 84, 118-19; X, 92-93; XI, 86-87; XII, 147-48, 191-93, 241-42; XIII, 304-6, 357-59; XIV, 102-3, 136-38, 202-7, 210-11, 236, 316-17; XV, 15, 32-35, 53-56, 96-97, 109-12, 128-30, 143-45, 220-23, 231-34.

32 *Ibid.*, VII, 178-80.

33 *Ibid.*, XV, 53-56.

an element of sexual exploitation which disturbed the conscience of the community. This explains in part the reluctance of masters to legitimize offspring for whom they obviously felt deep affection. Religion, on the other hand, carried no illicit taint; rather, it was respectable and, superficially at least, provided a point of contact between the races not blighted by exploitation. It is not surprising therefore that attempts to indoctrinate the slaves in the religious beliefs of the whites not only had wide support but reassured the whites of their own moral superiority. And the colonial authorities were strongly in favor of proselytization, for they equated Christianity with civil stability.[34] As early as 1686 Governor Dongan was instructed by England "to find out the best means to facilitate and encourage the conversion of Negroes."[35] Many slaveholders proselytized their bondsmen, at least to the extent of bringing them to religious services and encouraging them to conform outwardly to Christianity.[36]

The masters, however, were generally unwilling to have their slaves indoctrinated by anyone but themselves. They did not want them to receive catechetical instruction from either clergy or lay preachers, for they were morbidly suspicious of activities affecting their slaves over which they did not have direct personal control.[37] Thus it is not surprising that the main impetus to organized proselytization came not from the slaveholders but from a missionary group in England known as the Society for the Propagation of the Gospel in

[34] *N.Y. Eccles. Recs.*, II, 916, 954, 1034; *Cal. State Papers, Col.*, XVII (1699), 176.
[35] *N.Y. Col. Docs.*, III, 374.
[36] *N.Y. Eccles. Recs.*, I, 489.
[37] Humphreys, *Account of the Endeavours by the S.P.G.*, pp. 9-10. See also Morgan Dix, *A History of the Parish of Trinity Church* (New York: vols. I-IV, The Knickerbocker Press; vol. V, Columbia University Press, 1898-1950), I, 349-50.

Foreign Parts. This organization had the support of the highest civil and ecclesiastical officials in England and was probably the most powerful branch of organized philanthropy in the eighteenth century.[38] Founded to save souls, both white and black, the S.P.G. provided much of the drive and most of the money behind the missionary effort in New York.[39]

For its overseas missions the S.P.G. recruited catechists in the communities which they were to serve so that their activities would not arouse suspicion or hostility among the local inhabitants. The S.P.G. was convinced that catechists with personal contacts in the community would be in the best possible position to win the support and cooperation of the slaveholding class. This was the principal reason for the appointment of Elias Neau, a respected merchant and close friend of Governor Hunter, to serve as catechist to the slaves of New York City.[40] The policy of making local appointments whenever possible was followed throughout the province. The S.P.G. enlisted the Anglican pastors of Jamaica, Rye, and New Rochelle, as well as the schoolmasters of Albany, Hempstead, and Staten Island, to give religious instruction to the bondsmen.[41] Everything

38 Humphreys, *Account of the Endeavours by the S.P.G.*, p. 3.

39 *Rev. and Misc. Papers*, III, 357. See Humphreys, *Account of the Endeavours by the S.P.G.*, p. 18.

40 *Rev. and Misc. Papers*, III, 349. See Dix, *History of Trinity Church*, I, 162.

41 Francis L. Hawks' Records of the General Convention of the Protestant Episcopal Church of New York, I, 635-37, MS. coll. N.Y. Hist. Soc.; Ernest Hawkins, *Historical Notices of the Missions of the Church of England in the North American Colonies, Previous to the Independence of the United States: Chiefly from the MS. Documents of the Society for the Propagation of the Gospel in Foreign Parts* (London: B. Fellowes, 1845), p. 273; Joseph Hooper, *A History of St. Peter's Church in the City of Albany* (Albany: Fort Orange Press, 1900), pp. 70-72. See C. E. Pierre, "The Work of the Society for the Propagation of the Gospel in Foreign Parts among the Negroes of the Colonies," *Journal of Negro History*, I (1916), 358-59.

that could be done was done to make the missionary
effort respectable and safe in the eyes of the masters.

The instruction provided by the S.P.G. was not
limited to religious indoctrination. Besides catechetical
instruction, the teachers employed by the S.P.G. ran
day and evening courses for slaves in reading and writing.[42] The classes held by John Beasly, the catechist at
Albany, were so popular that Beasly's home was crowded
at all hours of the day with Negroes seeking instruction.[43] In 1760 the S.P.G. opened a school at New York
City to provide Negro children with a rudimentary education. All the children attending were given instruction in reading, writing, and arithmetic; the girls were
given additional lessons in sewing.[44] The costs of instruction and books were covered by the S.P.G., which
requested the slaveholders only to provide wood to heat
the building during the winter months.[45]

The S.P.G. nevertheless encountered stubborn resistance to its activities in all parts of the province. Most
slaveholders were bitterly opposed to the indoctrination
of their slaves by professional proselytizers. Many of
them warned their slaves that they would be sold outside New York if they had anything to do with the
missionaries.[46] They preferred instead to indoctrinate
the slaves themselves in a safe version of Christianity
with dangerous ideas carefully deleted. Slaveholders
were well aware that some of the evangelical sects, particularly the Baptists and Quakers, preached an equali-
tarian gospel inimical to slaveholding. The hostility of
these sects toward slavery compromised even the con-

42 Hawks' Records, II, 9-10. See Hawkins, *Historical Notices of the Church of England*, p. 273.
43 Hooper, *History of St. Peter's Church*, pp. 70-72.
44 Dix, *History of Trinity Church*, I, 294-95.
45 *New York Mercury*, September 15, 1760.
46 Hawkins, *Historical Notices of the Church of England*, p. 271.

servative denominations in the eyes of the slaveholding class. Clergymen and lay catechists who attempted to proselytize slaves invariably aroused suspicion regardless of religious affiliation or standing in the community.[47]

Another reason for resistance to the missionary effort was the fear that formal conversion to Christianity might give the slaves a legal claim to freedom.[48] This fear sprang mainly from the fact that in colonial times civil status was tied closely to religion. The right to vote, to hold public office, and to own real property were all subject to religious tests. Moreover, the legal basis of slavery was somewhat unclear, for even after legalization it rested exclusively on local municipal law. Since the English common law did not recognize chattel bondage, the legal premises of the slave system were in fact extremely shaky.[49] Indeed, on some points the system conflicted directly with the common law. For one thing, the rule that the status of a child followed the status of its mother was borrowed from the civil law, not from the common law, which fixed status by paternal descent.[50] The uncertainty surrounding the legal status of slavery made masters morbidly suspicious of attempts to change the status of the bondsmen in any respect.

Slaveholders were also worried by the judicial decisions in England which equated civil status with religion. In several cases the courts held that no Christian could be kept in slavery regardless of race or prior con-

[47] *Ibid.*, pp. 50, 73.

[48] *Cal. State Papers, Col.*, XVII (1699), 176.

[49] William Goodell, *The American Slave Code* (New York: The American and Foreign Anti-Slavery Society, 1853), pp. 260-61; Hurd, *Law of Freedom and Bondage*, I, 278.

[50] *Col. Laws N.Y.*, I, 597-98. See George M. Stroud, *A Sketch of the Laws in Relation to Slavery in the United States of America* (Philadelphia: Kimber & Sharpless, 1827), pp. 2-3, 10-11.

dition of servitude.[51] Although these decisions were not strictly binding outside of England, they were a source of great anxiety to the master class. This anxiety was especially acute in New York, where the bungling of local officials created the impression that the colonial government favored the English rule. Carelessly drafted statutes and slipshod census taking seemingly equated Christianity with freedom. A statute of 1686, for example, outlawed the enslavement of Christians "except such who shall be judged thereto by authority, or such as willingly have sold or sell themselves."[52] This was meant to apply only to indentured servants, but imprecise draftsmanship gave it a more sweeping meaning. Likewise the census of 1712 identified the free population as the "Christian" population.[53] Obviously not every non-Christian was a slave nor was every Christian free, but the careless overlapping of categories implied a relation between religion and freedom.

With so much to feed their suspicions—the English decisions, ambiguous statutes, and equivocal census returns—it is easy to understand why so many slaveholders were hostile to any attempt to proselytize the slaves. Nothing could dissuade them from believing that the missionary effort was basically inimical to their interests. Even assurances from the Solicitor and Attorney General of England that their legal rights would not be impaired in any way failed to move them, for their anxiety was not confined to legal consequences alone.[54]

[51] The English rule was that Negroes could be held as slaves "until they become Christians and thereby they are enfranchised." See *Butts v. Penny*, 3 Kemble's Reports 785, 1 Lord Raymond's Reports 147.
[52] *Col. Laws N.Y.*, I, 18.
[53] *N.Y. Col. Docs.*, V, 339-40.
[54] Cobb, *Inquiry into the Law of Slavery*, pp. 153, 162. See *New York Packet*, April 25, 1788.

Many of them were convinced that any change brought about by the proselytizers—and this included the moral improvement of the slaves—would only work to undermine the slave system. One master in New York City pointed out that such improvement might fill the slaves with "dangerous conceits."[55] They might, for instance, be led to question the premises of a system which subjected them to morally inferior masters. Slaveholders did not forget for a moment that Christian slaves had played a leading role in the bloody insurrection of 1730 in Virginia. Many believed that proselytization had been responsible for the Virginia uprising, and even those who did not share this belief did not want to put the theory to a test in New York.[56]

In point of fact, however, the missionary effort was not nearly so dangerous as the slaveholders imagined. Most of the proselytizers employed by the S.P.G. were solid Anglicans with a stolid respect for things as they found them. Although they never apologized for slavery or acted as conscious lackeys of the master class, it is also true that they never questioned the premises of the system. Anglican missionaries were more concerned with liturgy and doctrine than with the secular implications of Christianity. They spent long hours drilling their Negro catechumens in religious orthodoxy. Slaves who underwent indoctrination by the S.P.G. were generally fed a bland diet of homiletics seasoned with occasional exhortations about the hereafter and the need for submission to lawful authority. The only remotely radical idea advanced by the missionaries was the brotherhood of all men under the Fatherhood of God. Certainly,

[55] Hawks' Records, I, 639. See Dix, *History of Trinity Church,* I, 185-86.
[56] Hawks' Records, II, 33-34.

however, none of the proselytizers ever attempted to equate Christianity with freedom or secular equality.[57]

There is no evidence which indicates that religious indoctrination caused discontent among the slaves. Indeed, all the evidence is to the contrary: that slaves who accepted Christianity were more submissive and adapted better to bondage than the non-Christians. The latter were responsible for numerous brawls, disorders, and even more serious threats to the public safety. The uprising of 1712, for instance, was organized and led by superstitious non-Christians who believed that heathen spells could make them invulnerable to the white man's bullets.[58] Christian slaves took no part at all in the conspiracy, a fact most gratifying to the missionaries.[59] One proselytizer seized upon the event to point out that all his converts had perfect records for orderly and sober living after conversion.[60] This does not mean that proselytization necessarily induced submissiveness, for it is possible that only the most docile slaves were attracted to Christianity in the first place. In either case the evidence is convincing that the proselytizers were not a threat to the slave system.

A difficult obstacle encountered by the S.P.G. was the extreme hostility of the dissenting denominations to any agency sponsored by the Church of England. Quakers would not permit their slaves to have any contact with S.P.G. proselytizers, and the Presbyterians, though they permitted instruction, would not allow

[57] Hawks' Records, I, 133-35; Humphreys, *Account of the Endeavours by the S.P.G.*, p. 5; N.Y. Eccles. Recs., III, 1559, 1609, 1613-14; Dix, *History of Trinity Church*, I, 162; Hawkins, *Historical Notices of the Church of England*, p. 272; *Rev. and Misc. Papers*, III, 348; William Berrian, *An Historical Sketch of Trinity Church* (New York: Stanford & Swords, 1847), pp. 35, 58-60.
[58] *Infra*, pp. 122-23.
[59] *Rev. and Misc. Papers*, III, 353.
[60] Berrian, *Historical Sketch of Trinity Church*, pp. 59-60.

their slaves to be baptized.[61] Anti-Anglican sentiment made it difficult for the S.P.G. to obtain financial support where it was most needed—at the local level.[62] Some proselytizers found that the hostility of the dissenters brought Anglicanism into disrepute among the slaves to such an extent that in some communities the missionary effort was foredoomed to failure.[63]

Another obstacle was the difficulty of reaching widely scattered slaves living on farms in the rural areas. One proselytizer found the slave population of Hempstead so widely dispersed that it was virtually impossible to bring more than a few Negroes together at the same time for instruction.[64] The same problem existed in Westchester and other country districts.[65] The Reverend Thomas Poyer reported to the S.P.G. that he could not even estimate the number of slaves living in his Jamaica parish.[66] Another proselytizer reported in 1729 that there were about one thousand slaves in Albany County with whom it was impossible to establish contact.[67] There can be no doubt that the difficulty of reaching slaves in the outlying areas seriously hampered the missionary effort.

What the slaves in turn thought of Christianity cannot be known directly, for they left no diaries or written records. Their attitude nevertheless can be inferred from their response to the missionaries, which by and large was negative. This apathy, rather than the opposition of the masters, was the main obstacle to the missionary effort. Even when the proselytizers somehow managed to win the confidence of individual slave-

---

61 Baird, *History of Rye*, p. 185.
62 Humphreys, *Account of the Endeavours by the S.P.G.*, p. 18.
63 Hawks' Records, I, 218-19.
64 *Ibid.*, II, 6-7, 9.
65 *Ibid.*, I, 693-94; II, 33-34.
66 *Ibid.*, I, 634.
67 *Ibid.*, II, 19-20.

75

holders, they could not long hold the interest of the slaves.[68] A missionary working in Albany County ruefully informed the S.P.G. that the slaves there displayed no interest at all in the Christian religion.[69] Only one slave in every ten in New York City was a Christian after a decade of the most intense missionary activity.[70] Results were just as bad in other parts of the province. Only fifty-three slaves were baptized in Huntington over a period of fifty-six years, a conversion rate of somewhat less than one slave per year—clear proof that the slaves were not won over in significant numbers.[71] In the township of Rye only one slave in every hundred was a Christian after ten years of proselytization.[72] From a statistical standpoint at least, such results must spell failure for the missionary effort.

One of the reasons the slaves did not respond more favorably to proselytization was their dissatisfaction with the secular aspects of Christianity. Not only did conversion fail to improve their everyday lives, but it subjected them to a moral discipline utterly incompatible with slavery. Some proselytizers admitted as much in their reports to the S.P.G. One catechist decried the hypocrisy of expecting the slaves to practice monogamy when their marital ties might be broken at any moment by the vagaries of slavery.[73] Christian mores were too remote from real life for the slave to take them seriously. The New York bondsman was much more sophisticated in this regard than his counterpart in the southern colonies. His contempt for hypocrisy caused him to

[68] Humphreys, *Account of the Endeavours by the S.P.G.*, p. 7.
[69] Hawks' Records, II, 19-20.
[70] *Rev. and Misc. Papers*, III, 356.
[71] Ebenezer Prime, ed., *Records of the First Church of Huntington, Long Island, 1723-1779* (Huntington: Moses L. Scudder, 1899).
[72] *N.Y. Eccles. Recs.*, III, 1695.
[73] *Rev. and Misc. Papers*, III, 350, 355.

reject religious formulas which could not be put into actual practice. One proselytizer mistakenly complained to the S.P.G. that the slaves "lacked the facility of understanding."[74] The truth is they understood only too well the impossibility of reconciling preachment with reality.

The missionary effort, however, did have the positive effect of focusing attention on the slave's spiritual and moral equality with the whites. Although most of the proselytizers carefully skirted the social implications of Christianity, some of them were more daring, at least to the extent of warning masters that they had a religious duty to treat their slaves as fellow human beings.[75] In all meetings sponsored by the S.P.G., whites and Negroes came together on terms of complete equality. The proselytizers and schoolmasters employed by the Society held fully integrated meetings in all parts of the province.[76] Moreover, whatever the arrangements, Negroes were admitted to white churches everywhere.[77] Organized religion was in fact the only institution which even pretended to treat free whites and Negro slaves as equals. Although most of the proselytizers were conservative clerics, they made no attempt to justify slavery by giving it religious sanction. They treated it in the only way that was possible in a slaveholding society: they ignored it and left it to the masters to rationalize as best they could.

Taken together, the missionary effort caused slavery much indirect harm. By asserting the spiritual equality of the slaves with the masters, the proselytizers struck a

74 Hawks' Records, I, 229, II, 33-34; Rev. and Misc. Papers, III, 355.
75 Humphreys, Account of the Endeavours by the S.P.G., pp. 28-30.
76 N.Y. Eccles. Recs., IV, 2357. See William T. Davis, C. Leng, and R. W. Vosburgh, The Church of St. Andrew, Richmond, Staten Island (New York: Staten Island Historical Society, 1925), pp. 29, 124.
77 N.Y. Eccles. Recs., III, 1613-14; Prime, ed., Records of the First Church of Huntington, passim. See Berrian, Historical Sketch of Trinity Church, pp. 117-18.

hard blow at the principal ideological basis of the system—the idea that it was justified by an inferiority of race. The proselytizers failed in their attempts to extend Christianity, for they won relatively few converts among the slaves. But they made a deep impression on the white population by insisting that the ultimate worth of a man had nothing to do with race or status. The open hostility of slaveowners to the missionary effort was motivated in part by an awareness that is was basically incompatible with slavery. Although the proselytizers never attacked the institution directly, they boldly asserted the slave's spiritual equality with the rest of the population.[78] This assertion was ultimately of far greater importance than the failure of the proselytizers to win converts. It was, as many of the slaveholders had feared, an opening to freedom.

[78] Humphreys, *Account of the Endeavours by the S.P.G.*, pp. 28-30.

V. SLAVE CONTROLS

> "AN ACT . . . FOR REGULATING SLAVES IS BE-
> COME ABSOLUTELY NECESSARY THROUGH THE
> GREAT INSOLENCY THAT SORT OF PEOPLE ARE
> GROWN TO."
>> —*Governor Cornbury to the Council of Trade,*
>> *March 5, 1702/3.*

B ASED on race from its beginnings in New Netherland, the slave system existed for several decades without express legal sanction. During this period of extralegal operation the institution functioned much like a system of indentured servitude under which Negro bondsmen were regarded not as chattels but as servants for life. In this respect the New York slave system followed a pattern typical of slavery in the other English colonies.[1] Although they belonged to a visibly different race, Negroes were treated the same as white indentured servants. Their status was not exactly the same of course, for they did not have indentures to define the terms of their service. It was taken for granted nevertheless that they were persons before the law and for several decades after the English occupation they were allowed to testify against whites in all the courts of New York.[2]

But because they belonged to a race which was not only visibly different but culturally primitive by Euro-

---

[1] Phillips, *American Negro Slavery*, pp. 75-77; Stampp, *The Peculiar Institution*, pp. 21-23.

[2] A. J. F. Van Laer, ed., *Minutes of the Court of Albany, Rensselaerswyck and Schenectady, 1668-1680* (Albany: University of the State of New York, 1926-28), II, 97, 122, 137, 168, 172, 179, 401, 417-18.

pean standards, it was easy and profitable to assume that Negro bondsmen had no rights which limited the power of the master class. The racial uniqueness of the Negro encouraged a trend toward special treatment which in the end reduced the bondsmen to chattels completely under the power of the masters. From 1682 onward the colonial government promulgated a wide variety of police statutes which expressly legalized slavery for persons of Negro blood. These statutes subjected Negro bondsmen to special public controls, disqualified them as witnesses against whites, and recognized the complete power of the masters over them.[3]

Doubtless this development was inevitable, for slavery could not have existed indefinitely without the physical coercion sufficient to compel the submission of the slaves. The system of course rested on naked force, for nothing could obscure the fact that the bondsmen hated slavery. Although few of them were openly rebellious, resistance to slavery was manifested in numerous ways. Some slaves resisted by running away or malingering, and most of them were eager to work at odd jobs during their leisure time in order to earn enough to buy their way to freedom. The most obvious fact about slavery is that every bondsman placed a high value on personal liberty.[4] It is not surprising therefore that the survival of the slave system required a large body of statute law and local ordinances to restrain the normal impulses of the bondsmen.

Because the ultimate form of resistance was insurrection, most of the public controls were aimed at restricting communication among the slaves. As early as 1682 it was a misdemeanor, punishable by flogging, for

3 *Proc. Gen. Ct. of Assizes,* pp. 37-38; *Col. Laws N.Y.,* I, 519-21, 597-98, 617-18, 631, 762-64.
4 Register of Manumissions, *passim.*

more than four slaves to meet together on their own time.[5] In 1702 the number permitted to meet together was reduced to three and, in order to insure uniform enforcement, each town was required to maintain a "Negro whipper" to flog violators.[6] Gambling was strictly prohibited in New York City and slaves over the age of fourteen had to be off the streets by sunset unless accompanied by a member of the master's family.[7] At Kingston the rule was that any "above the number of three Negroes found together upon the Lord's Day or at any unreasonable hours . . . shall be publicly whipped or the master to pay a fine of 8 shillings."[8] Hunting was forbidden in Westchester, and slaves in Smithtown were not allowed to travel more than a mile from home without a pass.[9]

The public regulations were supplemented by a system of private controls enforced by the master class. Legally the slaves were chattels which the masters might lend, lease, sell, or otherwise dispose of at any time. Short of death and mutilation, the law unconditionally upheld the right of the master to punish private offenses committed by his bondsmen and to use whatever force was needed to compel obedience. The ultimate sanction of slavery was force, and the law supported it completely in this respect. If a slave ran away, malingered, or disobeyed a command, he committed a private offense punishable by the master. How this power was used varied according to the character and temper of the master. But whether the master was cruel or kind was

[5] *Proc. Gen. Ct. of Assizes,* pp. 37-38.
[6] *Col. Laws N.Y.,* I, 519-21.
[7] *Minutes of the Common Council,* III, 277-78.
[8] Court of Sessions, Ulster County, Kingston, September 3, 4, 1695, Hist. Docs. Coll., Klapper Library, Queens College.
[9] Dixon Ryan Fox, ed., *Minutes of the Court of Sessions, 1657-1696, Westchester County* (White Plains: Westchester County Historical Society, 1924), pp. 66-67; Pelletreau, ed., *Records of Smithtown,* p. 170.

his own affair, for the law regarded the power of discipline as inseparable from the right of ownership.[10]

But the law was even more concerned with the safety of the community than with the rights or powers of the slaveholder. Although slaveholding was legally protected, the interests of the masters were not always compatible with the larger interests of the community. Because slaves were a dangerous form of property, the law held slaveowners responsible for any misconduct by their bondsmen.[11] Besides being civilly liable to private citizens for property damages, masters were threatened with fines for public offenses committed by their slaves.[12] In every instance, the protection and safety of the community had priority over the property rights of the masters.

The slave controls also created a class of crimes which white persons could commit with regard to slaves. These included acts likely to interfere with the owner's control of his slaves or likely to undermine discipline and threaten the public safety. The hiring of slaves without the express consent of the master was prohibited in New York City in order to prevent slaves from being hired away from their regular duties.[13] Both Albany and New York City had ordinances forbidding innkeepers to sell liquor to slaves or accept their patronage without the permission of the masters.[14] In Westchester County the taverns were forbidden to sell "any strong drink to Negroes without consent of their mas-

10 Cobb, *Inquiry into the Law of Slavery*, pp. 89-90.
11 *Col. Laws N.Y.*, I, 519-521.
12 *Proc. Gen. Ct. of Assizes*, pp. 37-38; *Minutes of the Common Council*, I, 134, 136-37; Fox, ed., *Minutes of the Court of Sessions*, pp. 66-67; Pelletreau, ed., *Records of Smithtown*, p. 170; Joel Munsell, ed., *Annals of Albany* (Albany: J. Munsell, 1859), VIII, 296.
13 *Minutes of the Common Council*, IV, 85.
14 *Ibid.*, I, 85-86; Munsell, ed., *Annals of Albany*, VII, 172.

ters."[15] These prohibitions against entertaining were extended by statute throughout the province by 1703.[16] Another statute forbade trading with slaves or accepting any goods or property from them without the master's consent. Persons who violated the law were guilty of a felony, and the failure of witnesses to report violations was made a misdemeanor.[17]

Illegal trade caused the masters great difficulty, for it was found that such trade encouraged theft. Slaves often pilfered goods, sometimes in large quantities, in order to obtain luxuries and entertainment normally beyond their reach.[18] One slaveholder in New York City discovered that his most trusted slave had broken into his warehouse and made off with much of its contents.[19] The law against illegal trading was vigorously enforced, even to the extent of offering rewards to informers who reported violations.[20] And the courts gave the law a strict interpretation by placing on the defendant the burden of proving that the slave with whom he had traded had been duly authorized by his master. Steven Valloau of Kingston was fined forty shillings for selling liquor to slaves despite his plea that he had done so in the belief that the masters had given their approval.[21] The mere act of trading with slaves was regarded as sufficient for a conviction unless the defendant could prove that the master had in fact given his consent.[22]

15 Fox, ed., *Minutes of the Court of Sessions*, p. 67.

16 *Minutes of the Supreme Court of Judicature, 1673-1701*, in New-York Historical Society, *Collections*, XLV (1912), 43, 113, 172, hereinafter cited as *Min. Sup. Ct. of Judicature; Proc. Gen. Ct. of Assizes*, pp. 37-38.

17 *Col. Laws N.Y.*, I, 519-21.

18 *Supra*, pp. 63-64.

19 *New York Weekly Post-Boy*, February 4, 1744/45.

20 *Minutes of the Common Council*, I, 85-86.

21 Court of Sessions, Ulster County, Kingston, September 7, 8, 1693, Hist. Docs. Coll., Klapper Library, Queens College.

22 *Ibid.*, September 1, 2, 1697/98.

Slave stealing was the most serious crime of all that a white person could commit with regard to slavery. The slave stealers—"Negro jockeys" as they were known in colonial times—were universally detested. Some owners offered larger rewards for the apprehension of the "jockey" or any accessories to the theft than for the return of the slave.[23] Since the crime usually required the collusion of the slave, slave stealers had to work their way into the slave's confidence. Often the bondsman would be enticed into running away with a white accomplice who would sell him in another town or perhaps even in another province. Since the pattern could be repeated many times over, the original crime was frequently compounded at the expense of whoever bought the absconding slave. Bondsmen were usually enticed into such schemes by promises of ultimate freedom and a share of the purchase money collected from unwary buyers.[24]

But the slave controls were much more concerned with offenses committed by the slaves, and these ranged in seriousness from petty mischief to capital crimes. Theft was the most common offense of all and in some ways was probably inseparable from the slave system.[25] Some slaves stole systematically in order to obtain luxuries not normally available to them. One master in Albany discovered to his chagrin that a trusted slave had been tapping the family cash box in order to purchase expensive clothing.[26] However petty, such offenses were

23 *New York Mercury*, September 22, 1777; August 24, 1778.

24 *New York Weekly Post-Boy*, October 15, 1753; *New York Mercury*, November 2, 1772; September 22, 1777; August 24, 1778; December 21, 1778; May 19, 1783.

25 *Minutes of the Common Council*, IV, 497. See De Voe, *The Market Book*, pp. 264-65, and Walter F. Prince, "New York Plot of 1741," Typescript in Coll. N.Y. Hist. Soc.

26 *New York Weekly Post-Boy*, April 15, 1762. See Munsell, ed., *Collections on the History of Albany*, II, 380-83.

disquieting, for they indicated that the slaves were discontented, at least to the extent of their living standards under slavery. The prevalence of theft kept the community on notice that the bondsmen were unreconciled with their lot under slavery.

Next to theft, arson was the most common crime committed by slaves and, except for insurrection and murder, it was the crime most feared by the white population. The destructiveness of fires in colonial times caused slaveowners to be extremely apprehensive of incendiarism. Every unexplained or suspicious fire was attributed by the whites to criminal or rebellious slaves.[27] There was ample reason for apprehension, for disgruntled slaves often used fire to give vent to their discontent. The fire which destroyed Albany in 1793 was started by a few slaves to settle a private grudge against an unpopular master.[28] Fire could also be used to conceal theft, and since theft was common the danger was great.[29] Even the severe penalty for arson—burning at the stake—did not discourage slaves from setting fire to buildings to conceal pilferage. The crime was so easy to commit and so difficult to prove that even capital punishment had little deterrent effect.[30]

The public control of slavery was always more difficult in New York City than in the rural areas where the slave population was more widely dispersed. The concentration of population afforded the slaves numerous opportunities to meet together in violation of the law.[31] Most New York City slaves were artisans who were rela-

27 *New York Weekly Journal*, January 17, 1736/37; February 22, 1741/42; *New York Weekly Post-Boy*, June 25, 1750; January 1, May 14, 1753; Munsell, ed., *Collections on the History of Albany*, II, 380-83.
28 Munsell, ed., *Collections on the History of Albany*, II, 380-81.
29 *New York Weekly Journal*, April 17, 1741.
30 *New York Weekly Post-Boy*, March 16, 1746/47.
31 De Voe, *The Market Book*, pp. 265-66.

tively free of supervision during their leisure time. Many of these slaves adopted an insolent attitude toward the white population utterly inconsistent with their status. Mayor Merritt was assaulted when he ordered a group of them to disperse in 1696.[32] And one of the first impressions Governor Cornbury formed of New York City was of the "great insolency" of the slaves.[33] Disorderly slaves broke the curfew nightly and disturbed the town with their pranks and drunken brawls.[34] They acquired a reputation for trouble-making which extended far beyond the city. Indeed, some of the towns on Long Island would not allow them to enter without a pass from the local authorities.[35]

New York City slaves were legally subject to an elaborate body of public controls. Adult slaves were not allowed in the streets at night, nor were they allowed to play games or congregate within the town limits under penalty of a flogging for each offense.[36] Even their burial was closely regulated. Slaves could not be buried at night and not more than twelve slaves were permitted to assemble for a burial.[37] Most of these regulations were poorly enforced, however, for the masters found it convenient to close their eyes to violations so long as their slaves rendered satisfactory service. The Supreme Court of Judicature singled New York City out for special criticism because of the ineffectual enforcement of the slave controls.[38] So indifferent were the owners to the public controls that the municipal council in 1738

32 Stokes, ed., *Iconography*, IV, 397.
33 *Cal. State Papers, Col.*, XXI (1702-3), 32.
34 Parish's Transcripts (1695-1713), p. 3; *New York Weekly Post-Boy*, February 10, 1763.
35 Henry R. Stiles, *A History of the City of Brooklyn* (New York: Pub. by subscription, 1867-70), I, 208.
36 *Minutes of the Common Council*, III, 277-78.
37 *Ibid.*, IV, 447.
38 *Min. Sup. Ct. of Judicature*, p. 192.

passed an ordinance making them liable for a fine for every infraction committed by their slaves.[39]

Many of the offenses committed by New York City slaves had their origins in the disorderly taverns which catered to Negro bondsmen. Although the law forbade tavernkeepers to entertain slaves, many groggeries openly flouted the law.[40] Moreover, many whites of the lower class turned their homes into illicit drinking places for the bondsmen.[41] These places together with the regular groggeries illegally serving slaves were a mainspring of crime, for most of the bondsmen had to steal in order to pay for their entertainment. In a message to the Assembly, Lieutenant Governor Colden condemned such "tippling houses" as "destructive to the morals of servants and slaves."[42] Stolen goods were traded in these dives for liquor and the companionship of prostitutes. How many of these places existed cannot be determined, but they were numerous enough to be described in 1742 by one local newspaper as "the principal bane and pest of the city."[43]

Probably the most serious problem of slave control in New York City was posed by Spanish Negroes sold into slavery as prize property during the intercolonial wars. Many of these Negroes were free subjects of Spain taken from captured Spanish warships. Instead of being held as ordinary prisoners of war, the Spanish Negroes were brought before the vice-admiralty court where they were invariably condemned as prize property and sold into slavery.[44] The outcome of such proceedings

39 *New York Weekly Journal*, March 6, 1737/38.
40 *Col. Laws N.Y.*, I, 519-21; *Proc. Gen. Ct. of Assizes*, pp. 37-38.
41 Richard B. Morris, ed., *Select Cases of the Mayor's Court*, p. 745.
42 Lincoln, ed., *Messages from the Governors*, I, 659-60.
43 *New York Weekly Journal*, August 9, 1742.
44 Charles M. Hough, ed., *Reports of Cases in the Vice Admiralty of the Province of New York and in the Court of Admiralty of the State of New York, 1715-1788* (New Haven: Yale University Press, 1925), *passim*.

was rarely in doubt. The court required the prisoners to rebut the presumption that as Negroes they were slaves despite the fact that under the circumstances most of them had no means of proving their real legal status. As Governor Hunter explained in a report to the Board of Trade in 1741, many Spanish prisoners were adjudicated slaves "by reason of their colour which is swarthy."[45]

Such captives were naturally filled with resentment at the injustice of their treatment and for the most part held themselves aloof from the rest of the slave population. Refusing to accept their condition as permanent and ready for any desperate measure that offered hope of freedom, some of them were involved in an abortive uprising in 1712 and a supposed Negro plot in 1741, both of which threw the entire province into a panic.[46] In 1749 several Spanish Negroes attempted to cut a sloop out of the New York City harbor and escape by sea.[47] In the same year, four Spanish Negroes held as slaves on another New York sloop, the *Polly,* murdered the crew and ran the ship aground at Dominica.[48]

How many free Spanish Negroes were enslaved in New York cannot be estimated precisely, for some privateers sold their Negro prisoners without waiting for the formality of a vice-admiralty proceeding. The number was large enough, however, to involve New York in a bitter and protracted dispute with Spanish colonial authorities.[49] The continuous enslavement of Spanish Negroes in the 1740's finally brought a sharp response from the governor of Hispaniola. A special emissary named Joseph Espinosa was sent to New York to demand the

45 *N.Y. Col. Docs.,* V, 342.
46 *Infra,* 122-23, 126-39.
47 *New York Weekly Post-Boy,* April 3, 1749.
48 *Ibid.,* January 23, 1748/49.
49 Parish's Transcripts (1729-60), pp. 3, 8-9, 14-15.

release of the captives. Espinosa warned that unless the Spanish Negroes were restored to freedom English prisoners of war would be treated as slaves in Hispaniola.[50] This threat brought prompt results. The provincial council appointed a committee to investigate the enslavement of Spanish prisoners and to report its findings to the vice-admiralty court. The council warned that "any delay may be of ill consequences to any English prisoners that may fall into the enemy's hands."[51] It is not surprising therefore that the committee lost little time finding in favor of the slaves. The committee was in fact a face-saving device intended to impress the Spanish emissary, for it was fear of retaliation—of the "ill consequences" to English prisoners of war—that determined its findings. In any case, on the basis of the report the vice-admiralty court reversed its original judgment and ordered the release of the Negroes.[52]

The white inhabitants of New York City regarded the enslavement of Spanish Negroes as dangerous as well as unjust. In 1688 the municipal council intervened to obtain the release of some prisoners about to be sold as prize property.[53] The Reverend John Sharpe, the British Army chaplain at New York City in 1712, denounced the treatment accorded to Negro prisoners of war as "contrary to the Laws of Arms and the custom of nations."[54] And perhaps more to the point, a local newspaper warned that such slaves would "always aim at their deliverance at any rate, as 'tis likely our freemen would were they in slavery among the Spaniards."[55] By

50 *Ibid.* (1740-47), p. 26.
51 *Ibid.*, p. 34.
52 Hough, ed., *Reports of Cases in Vice Admiralty*, pp. 29-31.
53 *Calendar of Council Minutes, 1668-1783* (Albany: University of the State of New York [New York State Library Bulletin No. 58], 1902), p. 61. Hereinafter cited as *Cal. Council Min.*
54 *Rev. and Misc. Papers*, III, 351.
55 *New York Weekly Post-Boy*, April 24, 1749.

the mid-eighteenth century such sentiments gained the ascendancy and the enslavement of Spanish Negroes virtually halted. No condemnations of prisoners of war were recorded by the vice-admiralty court after 1750.[56] Thus ended a practice that had long caused anxiety in the general community.

Though always disquieting to the white population, slave disorders caused the greatest anxiety during the intercolonial wars when the militia were away from their home communities. It was feared by many that the absence of the local fighting forces might embolden the slaves to rebel.[57] The white population was fully aware that the slaves desired freedom and that there were some slaves who would stop at nothing in order to obtain it. Many New Yorkers regarded the Negro bondsmen as a greater threat in time of war than the French. Lieutenant Governor De Lancey, normally an icy realist, warned that the slaves could be expected to revolt if the French made an attack on New York City.[58] To secure the city against insurrection, special patrols were organized to replace the absent militia.[59]

Fear that the slaves might rise in support of a French invasion was especially acute on eastern Long Island, where some of the French exiles from Acadia had been resettled. Many of these Acadians had established friendly relations with the Negro bondsmen— much too friendly indeed for the peace of mind of the English. Some feared that if the French landed the Acadians would incite the slaves to revolt.[60] Colonel Richard Floyd, who commanded the Suffolk County militia, warned that failure to keep the slaves under

[56] Hough, ed., *Reports of Cases in Vice Admiralty*, pp. 199-201.
[57] *New York Weekly Post-Boy*, September 29, 1755.
[58] *Ibid.*, February 10, 1755.
[59] *Cal. Council Min.*, p. 435.
[60] Parish's Transcripts (1729-60), pp. 16-17.

close surveillance could bring disaster on the whole district.[61] Such fears tended to wane in peacetime only to flare up again as soon as hostilities broke out anew. During King George's War a French-speaking slave stirred up so much anxiety that his harassed owner had to sell him out of the province at a loss.[62]

The ever-present fear of insurrection was reflected in the harshness of the penal code. Since the purpose of the law was to protect the community by any severity necessary, a double standard of justice existed for whites and Negroes.[63] Slaves charged with serious crimes were seldom admitted to bail; rather, they were usually ordered to "remain in gaol untill discharged by due courts of law."[64] A great number of offenses not capital when committed by whites were punishable by death when committed by a slave. Offenses committed by Negroes against whites were relentlessly prosecuted and punished, whereas similar offenses by whites against Negroes were either ignored by the authorities or dismissed by the courts.[65] Although the master was always interested in protecting his slaves against an unjust charge, the rule that no testimony of a slave could be taken in court against a white person made it extremely difficult to obtain justice in cases involving both slaves and whites.[66]

Even minor offenses committed by slaves were punished more severely than offenses committed by whites. Slaves could not be punished by depriving them of either property or freedom because they had neither to

61 Cal. Council Min., p. 435.
62 New York Weekly Post-Boy, September 5, 1747.
63 Cobb, Inquiry into the Law of Slavery, p. 91.
64 Court of General Sessions of the Peace, Ulster County, Kingston, November 4, 1740, Hist. Docs. Coll., Klapper Library, Queens College.
65 New York Weekly Post-Boy, October 28, 1751.
66 Col. Laws N.Y., I, 597-98.

lose; only some form of physical punishment was in fact relevant for slave offenders. Thus petty offenses punishable by a fine or imprisonment when committed by whites were punished by flogging if committed by a slave.[67] There was also a special class of punishments which was reserved only for bondsmen. Slaves arrested for drunkenness in New York City were punished with the water cure—"a plentiful dose of warm water and salt to operate as an emetic, and lamp oil as a purge."[68] In 1772 the sheriff was absolved of responsibility for the death of a slave to whom he had given the cure on the ground that he had only inflicted "the usual discipline" for the offense.[69] By way of contrast, the usual discipline for white offenders was a small fine.[70]

Nevertheless, slaves charged with serious crimes had the benefit of clearly defined judicial procedures which the courts strictly adhered to. In the case of capital offenses, the slave could be tried only after a preliminary examination had determined whether there was a prima-facie case against him. The actual trial was conducted in a court especially created for the purpose consisting of three or more justices of the peace and five freeholders.[71] These tribunals were regular courts of record which heard witnesses, examined the evidence, and in general maintained a punctilious regard for the procedural rights of the defendant.[72] Certainly the system was far different from the drumhead justice slaves often received in other colonies.[73] Even during the con-

---

[67] Parish's Transcripts (1688-1760), p. 24; *Col. Laws N.Y.*, I, 617-18; *New York Mercury*, November 20, 1758.
[68] *New York Weekly Post-Boy*, May 11, 1772.
[69] *Ibid.*
[70] *Col. Laws N.Y.*, I, 617-18.
[71] *Ibid.*, I, 762-64.
[72] Justices Court, Ulster County, Kingston, July 1, 1741, Hist. Docs. Coll., Klapper Library, Queens College.
[73] But cf. Goebel and Naughton, who state that "the usual practice

spiracy panics of 1712 and 1741 all the procedural safe-guards were scrupulously observed by the courts.[74]

In part, the slave controls were intended to protect the slaves against excessive brutality. The willful killing of a slave was a capital offense, and the statutes also forbade the deliberate maiming or mutilation of a slave.[75] But since the law allowed the master to use whatever force was needed to enforce his commands, it is doubtful whether the protective provisions saved many lives. In any event, the court records do not contain a single instance of prosecution for slave killing. When a bad-tempered resident of New York City beat his slave to death in 1736, the coroner's jury investigating the case piously attributed the slave's death to "the visitations of God."[76] Although the city council subsequently passed an ordinance forbidding masters to beat their slaves without the approval of a magistrate, it is doubtful whether this had any deterrent effect.[77] No one was ever prosecuted under the ordinance, nor is there any evidence that masters bothered to obtain judicial approval before punishing their slaves.

Although some brutality was perhaps inevitable, it is also true that such acts were the exception rather than the rule. Certainly the New York slave system was free of the systematic barbarity that existed in some of the plantation colonies.[78] The best evidence of this can be found in newspaper advertisements for fugitive slaves.

---

was to try them summarily." Julius Goebel, Jr., and T. Raymond Naughton, *Law Enforcement in Colonial New York* (New York: The Commonwealth Fund, 1944), p. 418. The court records do not lend much support to this view.

[74] *Infra*, pp. 124-25, 128-31.

[75] *Col. Laws N.Y.*, I, 519-21.

[76] *New York Weekly Journal*, January 5, 1735/36.

[77] *Ibid.*, March 13, 1737/38.

[78] Goodell, *The American Slave Code*, pp. 218-20; Cobb, *Inquiry into the Law of Slavery*, p. 114.

Among the numerous advertisements describing the appearance of runaways, no instance of branding or physical mutilation can be cited.[79] By way of contrast, fugitives from other colonies are described as branded, scarred, and cruelly mutilated.[80] Public opinion in New York discountenanced the ferocious punishments inflicted in other colonies. So opposed were most New Yorkers to physical brutality that some owners had to sell unruly slaves out of the province rather than take the disciplinary measures needed to bring them into line.[81] Except for flogging, which was also inflicted on free whites and which was not regarded as particularly harsh in colonial times, the punishments imposed on bondsmen were about as humane as the nature of slavery permitted.

But New Yorkers were not inclined to be lenient if a slave committed a crime of violence against the white community. Justices of the peace could inflict any punishment short of amputation or death for an assault on a white person.[82] A statute of 1708 ordered the sheriffs to flog any slave who disturbed the peace "any law, custom or usage to the contrary hereof in any ways notwithstanding."[83] For more serious offenses punishment was frankly terroristic and brutal. One of the worst crimes was the killing of a white person, and slaves who committed it could expect no mercy. A statute passed in

79 But cf. James Truslow Adams, *History of the Town of Southampton* (Bridgehampton: Hampton Press, 1918), p. 201. Adams states that slaves on Long Island were frequently branded, but he offers no evidence that the branding was actually done there. That there were branded slaves in New York is undeniable, but in most cases it can be shown that they had been branded before their arrival in the province.
80 Weyman's *New York Gazette*, June 14, 1762; *New York Mercury*, September 5, 1757; July 11, 1763; July 20, 1772; *New York Weekly Post-Boy*, March 15, 1756; August 29, 1757; June 26, 1766.
81 *Colden Papers*, I, 39.
82 Smith, *History of the Late Province of New York*, II, 61-62.
83 *Col. Laws N.Y.*, I, 617-18.

1706 empowered the courts to punish capital offenses committed by slaves "in such manner and with such circumstances as the aggravation and enormity of the crime shall merit."[84] The judges used this power freely to impose brutal punishments in cases where the offense was especially heinous. In 1707, for instance, two slaves were sentenced to death by torture for murdering a white family on Long Island. A witness to the executions recorded that the slaves "were put to all manner of torment possible." One of the culprits was hung alive in chains and partially impaled so that his death pains were prolonged for hours.[85] Though admittedly rare, such terroristic displays demonstrate that New Yorkers had ample capacity for ferocity when the safety of the white community was threatened.

This ferocity, however, was as much a product of the age as of slavery. The most brutal punishments inflicted on slaves in New York were not unlike those of the English common law. White persons as well as slaves were subject to barbarous legal punishments in colonial times. Terror was regarded as an essential deterrent to crime in general, not as a means of racial repression. Indeed, crimes by slaves against slaves were dealt with almost as harshly as crimes against whites. When a slave belonging to Pieter Crussel of Kingston killed another slave in 1696, the court sentenced him "to be hanged by the neck till he shall be dead, and to be cut with a knife in his throat and after to be hanged in a chain for an example of others."[86]

It is also true that the double standard of justice under slavery sometimes favored the slave, for not every

[84] *Ibid.*, I, 631.
[85] Valentine, *Manual* (1870), p. 765.
[86] Special Court of Kingston, January 7, 8, 1695/96, Hist. Docs. Coll., Klapper Library, Queens College.

capital crime was punishable by death if committed by a slave. Slaves convicted of stealing property valued at less than £5 were by statute not liable to the death penalty as were whites under the English common law.[87] To execute a slave was to destroy valuable property for which the master had to be compensated by the government.[88] Thus in practice even the most serious crimes, including homicide, were punishable not by death but by transportation out of the province.[89] In 1749 John Murry of New York City used his considerable influence to have the grand jury quash a charge that one of his slaves had raped a white woman.[90] The normal punishment for this crime would have been burning at the stake.[91] One slave convicted of felonious assault on a white inhabitant of Kingston was freed on condition that his master "shall pay a fine of five pounds to be employed for the use of the county."[92]

In general, the punishment meted out to slave offenders became increasingly mild with the passage of time, especially toward the end of the eighteenth century when slavery had begun to decline as an institution. This was true even in cases of serious crimes of violence against whites. The punishment for rape against a white woman provides an interesting case in point, for it is possible to compare the punishment meted out to slaves in two almost identical cases of attempted rape and murder. The first occurred in 1742 and the slave

87 *Col. Laws N.Y.*, I, 519-21. See *New York Weekly Post-Boy*, February 4, 1744/45.
88 Parish's Transcripts (1729-60), p. 34.
89 Recognizance Pursuant to the Condition of the Pardon of a Negro Man Slave Called Falmouth, November 28, 1770, Misc. Slavery MSS., N.Y. Hist. Soc.
90 *Colden Papers*, IV, 142.
91 *New York Gazette*, January 28, 1734.
92 Court of Sessions, Ulster County, Kingston, September 3, 4, 1695, Hist. Docs. Coll., Klapper Library, Queens College.

was burned at the stake; the second occurred in 1797 and the slave was only flogged.[93] The leniency shown in the latter case was consistent with the decline of slavery in the late eighteenth century and the disappearance of terroristic punishments designed to enforce slave discipline. It is significant that in the same year the New York slave was flogged, a slave in Virginia, where slavery continued to be an important institution, was castrated for the same offense.[94]

Although slaves were legally subject to a way of life which attempted to regulate their whole existence, their everyday lives were in fact scarcely affected by the laws. Most of the slave controls were patently unenforceable, for they did not make any allowance for the needs of the slaves as human beings. The laws to prevent slaves from meeting together, if enforced, would have left the bondsmen with lives devoid of friendship and family attachments. New York slavery differed in this regard from the southern plantation system which enabled slaves to form personal ties without ever leaving the master's estate. Slaveholding was so widely diffused on a petty scale in New York that the slave had to make his personal contacts outside the household or business of the master. Thus the effect of the slave controls was to make friendships and family attachments among slaves legally impossible. Such controls, however, were largely ignored, for most slaves preferred punishment of any sort to leading lives devoid of human contacts. Generally ignoring the controls, the local authorities responsible for their enforcement sensibly closed their eyes to orderly slave gatherings and peaceful violations of the curfew.[95]

[93] *New York Gazette,* January 28, 1734; *Farmer's Oracle,* October 3, 1797.

[94] *Farmer's Oracle,* October 3, 1797.

[95] *New York Gazette,* February 9, 1730/31; *New York Weekly Journal,* August 9, 1742.

97

At best, many of the laws merely created an illusion that the slaves were under firm control. This of course was important in a way because it gave the community some relief against the morbid fear of insurrection. On the other hand, it magnified the importance of slave crime out of all proportion to its real significance. Although the crime rate was probably higher among the white population, offenses committed by slaves received a disproportionate amount of publicity and caused much more excitement. When a slave got drunk, threw a snowball, or fell into a barrel, the event was sure to be reported in detail by the newspapers.[96] Why even petty offenses committed by slaves should cause the community to take fright is not difficult to understand. The reason of course is that the slave alone was expected to make trouble, and the whites therefore drew the worst inference from his every mischief. Corrosive insecurity was in fact the price every member of the community paid for slavery.

On balance, many of the fears felt by the community were justified by the nature of slavery. The white population was correct in believing that slave offenses had more dangerous implications than similar offenses committed by whites. Not that every slave offense was a conscious blow against slavery, for many slaves took to crime for no better reason than to buy liquor or the companionship of a prostitute. Nevertheless, every offense served to remind the whites that the slave alone had no reason to accept or conform to the social order. The logic of bondage made the slave an institutional rebel. Even while breaking the law, most white offenders at least accepted the basic values of society. Indeed, many of them broke the law simply to gain greater en-

[96] *New York Weekly Post-Boy*, April 1, 1751; February 10, 1763; April 25, 1765.

joyment of things valued by society. Only the slave had reason to reject everything—law and values alike. Thus every offense committed by the slave underscored his resistance to slavery. Even if he could not win freedom in this way, at least he made his bondage more costly and troublesome to the whites.

VI. FUGITIVE SLAVES

"RUN AWAY FROM THE SUBSCRIBER, A NEGRO
MAN BELONGING TO MR. ROBERT BENSON,
NAMED POMPEY, ABOUT 25 YEARS OF AGE. . . .
HE HAS BEEN SKULKING ABOUT THE DOCKS
EVER SINCE HIS RUNNING AWAY, AND WANTS
TO GO A PRIVATEERING. THIS IS TO FOREWARN
ALL PERSONS FROM HARBORING SAID NEGRO
AT THEIR PERIL."
—*New York Weekly Post-Boy, July 26, 1756.*

F ROM the very beginning runaway slaves
made slavery an inconvenient and expensive system of
labor.[1] The desire for freedom was foremost in the mind
of every Negro regardless of the rigor or relative ease of
his bondage. Most of the slave population stubbornly
refused to accept bondage as a permanent condition of
life. The hope of gaining freedom inspired numerous
slaves to become runaways despite the many perils and
hardships a fugitive could expect to encounter.[2] Not
only bold or especially adventurous bondsmen made
the hard decision to run away. Even the most docile
and seemingly complaisant slaves were likely to become
runaways when the chances of winning permanent freedom seemed to outweigh the likelihood of being re-
captured.[3]

The forest wilderness was a favorite place of escape

[1] *Supra*, pp. 21-22.
[2] *New York Gazette* (1726-34); *New York Weekly Journal* (1734-43);
New York Weekly Post-Boy (1743-73); *New York Mercury* (1752-83).
[3] *Lloyd Papers*, I, 144. See Valentine, *Manual* (1865), p. 812.

for many runaways. Negroes who took to the woods often received assistance and asylum from the Indians. Numerous runaways in northern New York found refuge among the Senecas and Onondagas.[4] The Minisinks of eastern Long Island not only granted Negroes asylum but often welcomed them into the tribe.[5] The best evidence of the friendly attitude of the Indians toward runaway slaves can be found in the recovery clauses included in treaties between the province and the various Indian tribes.[6] Large rewards were regularly offered to induce the Indians to cooperate in the recovery of runaways.[7] But neither treaties nor the offer of rewards could dissuade the Indians from aiding slaves who fled to the forest. Even tribes as staunchly allied to the English as the Iroquois refused to surrender Negroes who took refuge with them.[8] Though some tribes like the Hurons, under pressure from the whites, promised to return runaways, there is no evidence that such promises were ever kept.[9]

How many slaves found refuge among the tribes is difficult to determine, but the number was large enough to alarm the provincial government. What the authorities feared was that the runaways might exert a dangerous influence on their Indian friends. The possibility that disgruntled slaves might incite the Indians against the whites was especially disturbing to the military au-

---

[4] Evert Wendell's Account Book (1695-1726), pp. 56, 89; Versteeg's Notes, pp. 14, 16. Both in MS. coll. N.Y. Hist. Soc.

[5] Kenneth W. Porter, "Relations between Negroes and Indians," *Journal of Negro History*, XVII (1932), 308.

[6] *Ibid.*

[7] *Colden Papers*, VII, 29-31.

[8] Franklin B. Hough, ed., *Proceedings of the Commissioners of Indian Affairs Appointed by Law for the Extinguishment of Indian Titles in the State of New York* (Albany: J. Munsell, 1861), I, 76-77.

[9] Porter, *Journal of Negro History*, XVII (1932), 308.

FUGITIVE SLAVES

thorities who were responsible for Indian affairs.[10] In the 1760's one of the runaway slaves living among the Mohawks stirred up so much trouble that the British Army had to reinforce its frontier garrisons.[11] When the Negro was finally captured in 1765, General Gage personally ordered him to be sold out of the province "so that he may never have an opportunity of getting among the Indians again."[12]

The Negro fugitives who took refuge among the Indians often intermarried with their hosts and lived out their lives with the tribes. Since the Negroes were outnumbered, they were easily assimilated into the tribes and their descendants soon lost their racial identity.[13] Within a generation, the descendants of these fugitives ceased to be Negroes and became Indians in outlook, culture, and racial composition. This fusion of Negro and Indian blood was continual throughout the colonial period. It is therefore difficult to estimate the number of Negroes living among the Indians, for many who were visibly Indians were of Negro ancestry. Such fugitives obtained the freedom they sought, but only at the cost of racial oblivion for their descendants.[14]

Some fugitives established camps in the wilderness and attempted to live by pilferage and raiding. In 1702 a band of runaways caused so much trouble on Long Island that Governor Cornbury ordered the local authorities to "fire on them, kill or destroy them, if they

10 J. Wickham Case, ed., *Southold Town Records* (New York: S. W. Green's Sons, 1882-84), I, 154, II, 74-75, 179; *Southampton Town Records*, IV, 9; *Papers of Sir William Johnson* (Albany: University of the State of New York, 1921-53), IX, 37; *Colden Papers*, IV, 166-68.

11 *Colden Papers*, VII, 46-47.

12 *New York Weekly Post-Boy*, July 18, 1765.

13 Porter, *Journal of Negro History*, XVII (1932), 308.

14 Melville J. Herskovits, "The American Negro Evolving a New Physical Type," *Current History*, XXIV (1926), 898-903.

103

cannot otherwise be taken."[15] Another band of slaves in Dutchess County in the 1750's supplemented the food which they raised in the forest by raiding nearby farms. Since they were not well armed, their forays were usually directed against chicken coops and barns and did not seriously threaten the white population. The whites were nevertheless alarmed by the raids and made several attempts to discover the slaves' camp. But every attempt failed, for the camp was well hidden and the slaves were too crafty to fall into any of the traps set for them by the whites. When the slaves finally disappeared from the county, it was generally assumed that they had attempted to make the trek north to Canada.[16]

Most of the fugitives who ran away in quest of permanent freedom attempted to get out of the province completely. Slaves living on the northern frontier usually tried to reach Canada in the hope of obtaining asylum among the French. Indeed, Anglo-French rivalry caused slaves on both sides of the frontier to seek freedom with the enemies of their masters.[17] Slaves who fled to Canada were far more dangerous to the province than those who joined the Indians or set up camps in the forest, for they were able to provide the French with information about the condition of New York's defenses. To halt the flight of slaves to Canada, the Assembly enacted a law in 1705 imposing the death penalty on slaves captured more than forty miles north of Albany.[18] The masters were to be compensated for slaves executed under this statute. The purpose of the law, made perma-

---

[15] Quoted in Herbert Aptheker, *Negro Slave Revolts in the United States* (New York: International Publishing Co., 1939), p. 72. See also Stephen M. Ostrander, *A History of the City of Brooklyn and Kings County* (Brooklyn: Pub. by subscription, 1894), I, 171-72.

[16] *New York Weekly Post-Boy*, October 29, 1753.

[17] Parish's Transcripts (1729-60), p. 3.

[18] *Col. Laws N.Y.*, I, 582.

nent in 1715, was not to deter slaves from running away but to prevent military information from reaching the French.[19] Only those slaves trying to reach Canada were subject to its penalties. Although many slaves attempted to reach Canada in spite of the law, an even greater number fled to New York City. A bustling port with a large transient population, the city provided an excellent hideout for runaways wishing to leave the province completely.[20] There were excellent opportunities of getting passage on an outgoing ship, for many captains were not overscrupulous in recruiting their crews.[21] Both male and female slaves gravitated to the waterfront hoping for a chance to escape the reach of their masters.[22] Indeed, it was generally taken for granted that runaways would attempt to escape by sea. The newspapers were filled with advertisements warning captains that they would be liable to civil and criminal prosecution if they assisted runaways in any way.[23]

There were never enough ships to accommodate all the slaves who fled to New York City. Some of the more desperate runaways seized sloops and ketches in which they attempted to make their escape from the province.[24] Others skulked along the waterfront, where they were

19 *Ibid.*, I, 880.

20 *New York Weekly Post-Boy*, September 16, 1751; June 18, 1753; February 27, July 3, October 3, 1758.

21 *New York Mercury*, July 13, 1761; May 31, September 27, 1762; May 16, 1774; May 4, 1778; March 1, September 13, 1779; October 1, 1781; June 10, 17, December 30, 1782; *New York Weekly Post-Boy*, May 25, 1747; June 18, 1753; November 4, 1775.

22 *New York Weekly Post-Boy*, July 26, 1756; *New York Mercury*, February 20, 1764; May 4, 1778.

23 *New York Mercury*, December 23, 1754; January 6, 13, 1755; June 4, August 13, September 24, 1759; March 17, April 14, May 5, 26, August 4, September 15, December 19, 1760; February 16, July 20, August 3, November 30, December 7, 14, 1761, *et seq.*

24 *New York Weekly Post-Boy*, November 15, 1764.

drawn into the gangs of criminal slaves infesting the docks. The most notorious gang was the Geneva Club, named after the Geneva gin its members were fond of imbibing. There were also groups known as the Free Masons, the Smith Fly Boys, the Long Bridge Boys, and many others whose names have not been recorded.[25] Slaves belonging to such gangs were extremely clannish and often engaged in murderous feuds.[26] Only rarely, however, did they attack white persons. The very existence of such groups nevertheless caused the whites much anxiety. The authorities regarded them as a much greater threat to the public safety than the deadlier gangs of white hoodlums on the waterfront.[27]

Runaways were generally younger slaves, mostly under the age of thirty, though occasionally older slaves would make the break for freedom.[28] Newspaper advertisements indicate that young men between the ages of eighteen and thirty accounted for about 80 per cent of all runaways in the eighteenth century.[29] The odds were heavily against women whether they fled to the forest or tried to escape by sea. Slave children normally did not become fugitives. Unaware of the full implications of slavery, they had no immediate motive for running away. Only in the late 1770's when the Revolution had strained slave relations to the breaking point did the number of children listed as runaways become significant.[30] But even then only youngsters who were old

25 De Voe, *The Market Book*, pp. 264-65.

26 *New York Mercury*, February 2, 1761.

27 Aptheker, *Negro Slave Revolts*, 72, 168-69.

28 *New York Weekly Post-Boy, February* 5, 1753; October 1, 1759; *New York Mercury*, June 26, 1758; October 1, 1759; August 30, 1762; September 12, 1763; January 29, 1770; August 26, 1776; June 30, 1779; August 11, 1783.

29 *New York Gazette* (1726-34); *New York Weekly Journal* (1734-43); *New York Weekly Post-Boy* (1743-73); *New York Mercury* (1752-83).

30 *New York Gazette* (1726-34); *New York Weekly Journal* (1734-43);

enough to shift for themselves were likely to make the break.[31] During the whole of the eighteenth century only one slave under the age of ten was recorded as a fugitive.[32]

Older slaves were even less likely to run away. Newspaper advertisements for fugitives reveal that only six slaves over the age of fifty were sought as runaways in the eighteenth century.[33] Even making allowance for masters who did not bother to advertise, the number of older fugitives is still negligible. The reason is fairly obvious. Elderly slaves usually lacked the physical stamina and incentive needed to become fugitives. Both were needed, but lack of incentive was probably the major factor. A long record of loyal service with the same master was usually sufficient to assure an older slave a comfortable living in his declining years. There were exceptions of course, for a sudden desire for freedom might manifest itself in slaves of any age.[34] On balance, however, the evidence is convincing that older slaves were inclined to remain at home.

The slaves who became fugitives represented a cross section of the slave population. Domestics and skilled artisans—the ones with apparently the closest ties with the master class—ran away as did field hands and common laborers. The list of runaways includes sailors, coopers, carpenters, butchers, tailors, bakers,

---

New York Weekly Post-Boy (1743-73); New York Mercury (1752-83); Weyman's New York Gazette (1759-67); New York Gazetteer (1783-87).

31 New York Mercury, October 25, 1756; January 15, 1759; March 10, June 16, 1760; October 11, 1773; August 26, 1776; February 10, 17, September 22, 1777; September 27, December 20, 1779; August 28, October 23, 1780; July 16, October 8, 1781; May 6, 1782; November 10, 1783.

32 Ibid., January 27, 1777.

33 New York Journal & Patriotic Register, August 15, 1795; Frothingham's Long Island Herald, June 7, 1791; New York Mercury, August 24, 1761; October 17, 1763; August 5, 1765; March 17, 1777.

34 Frothingham's Long Island Herald, June 7, 1791.

A History of Negro Slavery in New York

goldsmiths, tanners, shoemakers, blacksmiths, and chimney sweeps.[35] It is clear from this occupational spectrum that many of these slaves did not run away to escape privation or menial drudgery. Such a motivation might have been decisive for chimney sweeps and field hands but certainly not for the skilled workers who make up most of the list. Nor is there any evidence that the runaways were underfed, overworked, or treated with special cruelty. Indeed, most of the evidence available indicates the opposite: that the slaves by and large were treated humanely.[36] What every fugitive apparently had in common was revulsion for a life of bondage. It was the nature of slavery rather than special incidents in its practice that led slaves of all types to make the break for freedom.

When slaves sought freedom by running away, they usually had a clear grievance or objective to trigger their rebellion. One of the most common grievances was that of being separated from friends and family by sale to a master who lived in another part of the province. The desire to regain such lost relationships was often more than a displaced slave could bear.[37] Such slaves frequently became fugitives in order to return to their former homes. Runaways often concealed themselves in the neighborhood of their former masters in order to be near wives and families from whom they

35 *New York Weekly Journal,* May 10, 1736; *New York Weekly Post-Boy,* September 4, 1749; February 11, 1750/51; May 11, 1752; August 30, 1756; May 8, July 24, 1758; *New York Mercury,* July 18, 1757; May 22, 1758; December 12, 1763; May 16, 1774; March 17, 1777; August 29, 1779; September 6, 27, 1779; *New York Journal and State Gazette,* July 15, 1784; *New York Morning Post,* October 15, 1787.
36 *Supra,* pp. 61-63.
37 *New York Weekly Post-Boy,* June 12, 1749; January 8, 1749/50; April 23, 1753; January 1, February 19, 1761; August 23, 1764; December 5, 1765; February 20, 1766; August 13, 1767; *New York Mercury,* October 12, November 30, 1772; June 30, 1777; July 23, 1781.

had been separated by sale.[38] The perseverance of these fugitives was often astonishing. Some of them made their way back to their families from as far away as Virginia and South Carolina.[39]

The best evidence of the affection that bound many slave families together can be found in the advertisements for fugitives. One master on Long Island sought the return of a fugitive who had run away in pursuit of his wife, who had been sold to a buyer in the northern part of the province.[40] Another master was convinced that his runaway was hiding in the neighborhood "where he had a wife and children."[41] Even when they hoped to escape from the province completely, men often took along their wives and children, though this seriously lessened their chances of getting away.[42] One fugitive fled from Westchester County with his wife and two children.[43] Another took along his wife and four children.[44] One master in Eastchester advertised for a fugitive accompanied by a wife "in an advanced state of pregnancy."[45] It is clear that to many of these fugitives the attachments of the family were as important as freedom itself.

In most cases the runaways remained at large only a short time before they were caught or decided to return voluntarily. Slaves needed more than a fair share of luck and ingenuity in order to gain permanent freedom.

[38] *New York Weekly Post-Boy*, January 14, 1750/51; *New York Mercury*, September 16, 1771; January 11, 1773; *New York Journal & Patriotic Register*, May 7, 1794.
[39] *New York Mercury*, December 4, 1780.
[40] *Ibid.*, September 16, 1771.
[41] *New York Weekly Post-Boy*, April 23, 1753.
[42] *New York Mercury*, October 8, 1759; November 12, 1781; *New York Weekly Post-Boy*, November 14, 1748; May 31, July 5, 1756.
[43] *New York Mercury*, June 30, 1777.
[44] *New York Weekly Post-Boy*, November 14, 1748.
[45] *New York Mercury*, October 21, 1755.

Since strange Negroes generally aroused suspicion in colonial times, a fugitive had to be clever enough to give a plausible account of himself as he moved about the province. Lapse of time brought no real security, for some fugitives continued to be sought years after they had run away.[46] Slaves imported directly from Africa had an especially difficult time surmounting the language barrier if they became fugitives. Inability to speak English was enough to bring about the arrest of a Negro who wandered into a strange neighborhood.[47] Slaves able to speak English were at least able to fabricate cover stories when questioned by the authorities.

Some fugitives, relying on their light complexions, tried the bold approach when they reached a new community. Mulattoes of light pigmentation were often able to pass for white and thus lose themselves in the free population.[48] Even those unable to pass for white had an advantage over fugitives of darker complexion. Newspaper advertisements make it clear that such slaves were generally more difficult to recapture. Apparently they did not arouse as much suspicion as pure Africans on entering a strange community. But it is not true that most of the fugitives were mulattoes or of predominantly white ancestry. While this group was well represented, they were outnumbered by fugitives described in the advertisements as "black" or of seemingly predominant African ancestry.[49]

46 *New York Weekly Post-Boy*, January 8, 1762; *New York Mercury*, July 1, 1776.
47 *New York Weekly Post-Boy*, August 19, 1751; *New York Mercury*, November 9, 1761; October 11, 1762; June 17, 1765; October 29, 1770.
48 *New York Weekly Post-Boy*, August 27, 1759; June 18, 1761; March 18, 1771; *New York Mercury*, July 17, 1758; June 15, 1761; May 10, August 30, 1762; October 10, 1763; November 19, 1764; July 20, 1772; October 12, 1776.
49 *New York Gazette* (1726-34); *New York Weekly Journal* (1734-43); *New York Weekly Post-Boy* (1743-73); *New York Mercury* (1752-83).

Perhaps the most desperate of all those who made the break for freedom were the free Spanish Negroes sold into slavery by the court of vice-admiralty.[50] Burning with resentment at the injustice of their treatment, the Spanish Negroes stubbornly refused to accept their condition as permanent. For them no measure that offered the slightest hope of regaining freedom was too desperate.[51] Their resentment and obvious desperation caused many to fear for the safety of New York City. One newspaper warned that the white inhabitants "may one time or other feel the dreadful effect of their treacherous schemes in firing our town or some other bad adventures."[52]

The Spanish Negroes who fled faced the same difficulties as the Africans, for their accents were almost certain to give then away. Indeed, the problems facing fugitives were such that only slaves who had the foresight to invent a plausible cover story in advance had much chance of getting away. Some patiently bided their time until they could obtain a pass which would enable them to travel without arousing suspicion.[53] Such passes were issued by masters whenever it was necessary to send bondsmen any distance from home. The purpose of the pass was to identify the slave and explain the reason for his presence in a different part of the province. Such a pass provided the very best cover, so much so that the mere issuance of one could inspire a seemingly docile slave to run away.[54]

50 *Supra*, pp. 87-90.
51 *New York Weekly Post-Boy*, January 23, 1748/49; April 3, 1749.
52 *Ibid.*, April 24, 1749.
53 *New York Mercury*, April 23, 1753; June 24, 1754; May 22, 1758; January 19, 1761; January 23, September 3, 1764; June 8, 1772; April 5, 1773; July 29, 1776; *New York Weekly Post-Boy*, January 24, May 9, 1757; August 21, 1758; October 23, 1760.
54 *New York Weekly Post-Boy*, August 27, 1750; April 23, 1753; *New York Mercury*, June 12, 1758; January 23, 1764.

Slaves unable to obtain real passes sometimes managed to obtain bogus ones before running away. They were frequently assisted in this by both literate bondsmen and free Negroes.[55] Free Negroes often fed and concealed runaways, and the masters were powerless to do anything about it. Such assistance greatly increased the difficulty and expense of recapturing runaways.[56] Though deeply annoyed by the assistance given to fugitives by the free Negroes, slaveholders reserved their worst enmity for whites who provided runaways with bogus passes and false certificates of manumission. Some masters were more eager to punish such accomplices than to recover the fugitives. Newspaper advertisements were run warning that anyone who assisted a runaway would be subject to civil and criminal prosecution. In some cases larger rewards were offered for the arrest of the accomplice than for the return of the runaway.[57]

But even with a pass a fugitive had to be exceedingly clever to remain at large very long. For one thing, there were no antislavery organizations to assist him in colonial times. Nevertheless, there were some who managed to elude their masters and hoodwink the authorities with amazing success. The numerous runaways who made good their escape did so largely through their own intelligence and resourcefulness. The masters admitted as much in their advertisements for runaways. They warned the public that their runaways were "artful," "insinuating," "plausible," and "bright."[58] If correct, and there is no reason to doubt their accuracy,

[55] *New York Weekly Post-Boy*, August 19, 1751; *New York Mercury*, October 8, 1759; February 9, 1761; October 27, 1783.

[56] *New York Weekly Post-Boy*, October 23, November 5, 1753; June 27, 1765; *New York Mercury*, November 16, 1761; October 15, 1770; June 24, 1771; April 20, 1778; July 26, 1779; September 25, 1780.

[57] *New York Mercury*, April 5, 1773.

[58] *Ibid.*, January 18, 1762; July 4, 1763; January 20, 1772.

these appraisals indicate that many of the fugitives gave a remarkably good account of themselves.

Many slaves planned their break for freedom carefully, laying away money and supplies before running away.[59] One resourceful slave, pretending to act for his master, hired a horse which he charged to his master's account in order to speed his escape.[60] Artisans usually took along the tools which would enable them to earn a livelihood in the free life they hoped to make for themselves.[61] Some slaves, however, burdened themselves with useless articles that must have hindered their flight. One fugitive from Brooklyn ran away with two sheep and a beehive full of honey.[62] Another from Long Island took along his bed.[63] While the desire of the runaway to keep the few things that he could call his own is understandable, it is also clear that in some cases he thereby reduced his chances of getting away. Fugitives carrying beehives and beds attracted attention, a terrible liability in an enterprise where success depended upon remaining inconspicuous.

How much assistance runaways received from whites is hard to determine, but the complaints voiced by slaveholders indicate that it was considerable.[64] Fugitives often obtained asylum with employers in need of cheap labor. Farmers made use of runaways, especially at harvest time, and sometimes hurried them off without

59 *New York Weekly Post-Boy*, July 11, 1748; July 1, 1751; September 16, 1754; April 14, 1755; February 27, 1764; November 5, 1770.
60 *Ibid.*, June 21, 1764.
61 *New York Gazette*, August 27, 1733.
62 *Poughkeepsie Journal*, December 22, 1789.
63 *New York Weekly Post-Boy*, August 26, 1751.
64 *New York Gazette*, May 1, 1732; *New York Weekly Post-Boy*, May 24, 1756; August 1, 1757; July 3, 17, 1758; April 2, August 20, 1759; June 16, 1760; January 1, June 18, July 23, 1761; January 14, September 2, 1762; *New York Mercury*, June 4, August 13, September 24, 1759; March 17, April 14, May 5, 26, August 4, September 8, 15, December 29, 1760; February 16, July 20, 1761; December 12, 1763.

any pay at all. Employers not only used the services of runaways but often provided them with bogus passes so that they could move about more freely. Though slaveholders were well aware of such practices, they were powerless to prevent them. All they could do was to advertise for the return of runaways and offer rewards for information about whites who harbored their slaves or profited from their labor.[65]

The rewards offered by slaveholders for fugitives generally had no relation to the intrinsic value of the slave. Rewards for lost or fugitive property were nominal in the eighteenth century, and the usual reward was forty shillings whether the owner was seeking the return of a horse, boat, apprentice, indentured servant, or a slave.[66] In the case of an unusually valuable slave an exception might be made and a larger reward offered; on the other hand, an owner was not likely to offer forty shillings if the slave was worth less. The largest reward for the return of a runaway was offered by William Brownejohn of New York City, who in 1759 offered £10 for a slave;[67] the smallest, a reward of six cents, was offered by Luther Pratt of Troy. Pratt was apparently in earnest, for he advertised the offer over a period of several months.[68]

Runaways from other provinces were apparently as eager to get into New York as New York fugitives were to get out. Slaves regularly fled to New York from New Jersey and Pennsylvania, as well as from more distant places like Bermuda, Maryland, Halifax, St.

[65] *New York Weekly Post-Boy*, January 1, 1761.
[66] *New York Mercury*, October 1, 1770; *New York Weekly Post-Boy*, December 28, 1741; January 11, 1747/48; January 20, 1763.
[67] *New York Mercury*, January 29, February 26, March 19, 1759.
[68] *Farmer's Oracle*, October 3, 10, 17, 24, November 7, 21, 28, December 5, 12, 1797.

Christopher, St. Croix, Newfoundland, and Virginia.[69] Most of these fugitives were maritime workers who deserted from ships trading with New York. Ship-jumping was commonplace in colonial times and New York as a leading port had more than a few jumpers.[70] Local agents were usually appointed by the owners to press for the return of such runaways.[71] The presence of these fugitives in the province greatly added to the problems of local control and made the apprehension of New York runaways more difficult.

The authorities had virtually unlimited power in dealing with fugitives. Although at the beginning of the English occupation it was regarded as necessary to obtain warrants before seizing suspected fugitives, this practice was soon abandoned.[72] By the beginning of the eighteenth century any Negro suspected of being a runaway was subject to arrest and detention without any legal formality. Because there was no provincial law dealing with fugitives, the local authorities were free to handle the problem as they saw fit. It was perhaps inevitable that this power should be used at times to deprive free Negroes of their liberty. One Negro in New York City was arrested in 1773 for no other reason than "because he had curious marks on his back."[73] Anyone suspected of being a runaway of course had the burden of proving that he was not a slave.[74] And the courts

[69] New York Gazette, June 11, August 6, September 24, 1733; May 6, 1734; New York Mercury, June 20, October 3, 1757; November 10, 1760; August 8, 1763; May 7, 1764; October 17, 1774.

[70] New York Mercury, September 5, 1757; January 11, 1762; October 15, 1770; July 26, 1773; June 12, 1775; January 20, June 30, 1777; August 2, 1779; December 17, 1781.

[71] New York Weekly Post-Boy, March 12, 1749/50; April 19, 1756; New York Mercury, April 19, 1756.

[72] Colonial Records: General Entries G, 1664-1665, in New York State Library Bulletin, History, No. 2 (1899), I, 116-17, 170.

[73] New York Mercury, April 12, 1773.

[74] Cobb, Inquiry into the Law of Slavery, p. 67.

adopted the rule that a Negro working for a white person who claimed him as a slave had the burden of disproving the claim.[75] All Negroes were presumptively slaves and those unable to prove that they were free were always in danger of losing their freedom.

Negroes suspected of being fugitives were usually committed to the local jail while advertisements were run requesting their owners to claim them. And when a claimant came forward, the suspect was surrendered to him with the barest legal formalities.[76] It was sufficient for the claimant to identify the suspect as his slave and reimburse the sheriff for the costs of arrest and detention.[77] Once arrested, a Negro had almost no chance of regaining his freedom. The reason for this is not hard to find. The release of a suspect meant that the sheriff would be out the cost of detention, so it is not surprising that only suspects able to offer incontrovertible proof that they were free were likely to be released. Even the failure of claimants to come forward did not guarantee release. So complete was the power of the local authorities, and so defenseless were Negroes in the face of this authority, that unclaimed suspects were sometimes sold into slavery to cover the cost of their detention.[78]

75 *Trongott v. Byers,* 5 Cowens New York Reports 480 (New York Supreme Court, 1826).

76 The claimant of a slave only had to obtain a writ of replevin in the form of *homine replegiando* directing the sheriff to surrender the suspect unless the latter was able to offer affirmative proof that he was a free man. This procedure was much simpler than the procedure of the civil law which placed the burden of proof on the claimant. See *Skinner v. Fleet,* 14 Johnson's Reports 263 (New York Supreme Court, 1817). Cf. Cobb, *Inquiry into the Law of Slavery,* p. 253.

77 *New York Weekly Post-Boy,* February 12, 1749/50; April 16, 1750; November 19, 1759; January 8, February 26, 1770; *New York Mercury,* November 9, 1761; March 5, 1770; March 8, 1773.

78 *New York Mercury,* October 22, 1770; March 8, April 12, 1773; *New York Gazetteer,* March 31, 1784.

How many fugitives succeeded in gaining permanent freedom is hard to determine. Most breaks for freedom doubtless ended in failure, which meant punishment for the slave and probably a more rigorous servitude in the future. The runaway could not consider himself safe even if he managed to escape from the province completely. Intercolonial rivalry did not operate in the runaway's favor as it had during the New Netherland period.[79] The closest comity existed among the English colonies with regard to the capture and return of fugitives. Since every colony had some slaves, there was no disposition anywhere to give asylum to runaways. Every slaveholder as a matter of self-interest cooperated in the return of runaway slaves. Unless able to escape to a non-English colony, fugitives were not beyond the reach of their masters. On the other hand, the frequent appeals of masters inviting runaways to return and be forgiven are convincing evidence that many slaves managed to gain permanent freedom.[80]

Runaways had a better chance of gaining permanent freedom after 1775 than at any previous time. During the Revolution numerous slaves deserted to the British, who followed a policy of granting freedom to any bondsmen who joined them.[81] Some of the fugitives were helped on the way to freedom by officers in the American forces who regarded slavery as incompatible with the ideals of the Revolution.[82] And the winning of independence abruptly ended the comity which had existed on the return of runaways. The Articles of Confederation made no provision for the extradition of fu-

---

79 *Supra,* pp. 21-22.
80 *New York Weekly Post-Boy,* April 25, 1757; *New York Mercury,* January 12, August 24, 1761; May 21, 1764; December 23, 1782; June 30, 1783.
81 *Infra,* pp. 154-55.
82 Winslow C. Watson, *Pioneer History of the Champlain Valley* (Albany: J. Munsell, 1863), pp. 182-84.

gitives who escaped from their state of domicile. This omission had serious implications for slavery in New York once neighboring states began to take steps toward immediate or gradual emancipation. The trend toward emancipation began in Vermont in 1777 with the adoption of a constitution which prohibited slavery.[83] Between 1777 and 1784 Pennsylvania, Massachusetts, Connecticut, and Rhode Island enacted laws which set slavery on the road to extinction.[84]

The emancipation movement raised for the first time the question of the status of fugitives who had reached free territory. Under the Articles of Confederation each state was free to make its own policy without regard to the laws of any other states. Thus when Massachusetts expressly granted asylum to runaways, the state became a magnet for fugitives from New York. There was in fact no legal way owners could recover fugitives who had escaped to Massachusetts. Those who attempted to recover their slaves forcibly were subject to criminal prosecution.[85] Even after interstate comity was established under the Constitution of 1787, it was extremely difficult for owners to recover fugitives who had fled to other states. Although a slave-catching service was organized to return such slaves to New York, it is doubtful whether it met with much success.[86] The antislavery impulse of the late eighteenth century made slave catching unpopular, as well as expensive in view of the legal risks involved.[87] Most slaveholders there-

83 *Vermont Constitution of 1777*, Article I. See Hurd, *The Law of Freedom and Bondage*, II, 28.
84 *Laws of Pennsylvania, 1780*, CXLVI; *Acts and Laws of Connecticut, 1784*, pp. 233-34; *Acts and Resolves of Rhode Island, 1778*, pp. 14-15; *Massachusetts Constitution of 1780*, Article I.
85 Watson, *Pioneer History of Champlain Valley*, pp. 81-82.
86 *New York Journal & Patriotic Register*, January 16, 1799.
87 *William Dunlap's Diary*, in New-York Historical Society, *Collec-*

fore were content to write off their runaway bondsmen as permanent losses once they reached a free state.

---

tions, LXII-LXIV (1929-31), I, 119. Hereinafter cited as *Dunlap's Diary*.

VII. SLAVE
CONSPIRACIES

"THE LATE HELLISH ATTEMPT OF THE SLAVES
IS SUFFICIENT TO CONVINCE YOU OF THE NE-
CESSITY OF PUTTING THAT SORT OF MEN UN-
DER BETTER REGULATION BY SOME GOOD LAW
FOR THAT PURPOSE, AND TO TAKE AWAY THE
ROOT OF THAT EVIL TO ENCOURAGE THE IM-
PORTATION OF WHITE SERVANTS."
—*Governor Hunter to the Legislative Council,
May 1, 1721.*

EVERY slave who ran away did so out of discontent, and every sign of discontent reminded the
whites of the ever-present danger of insurrection. Most
of the towns had strict curfews, and throughout the
province there were stringent restrictions on the assembly and movement of slaves.[1] These measures were
frankly terroristic, for they authorized any degree of
punishment needed to deter conspiracy.[2] Even when
the slaves were seemingly docile, any hint or rumor of
conspiracy was sufficient to throw the whites into a
panic. Such rumors might be entirely unfounded, or
they might grow out of some incident magnified out of
all proportion by whites worried about conspiracy. A

[1] *Proc. Gen. Ct. of Assizes*, pp. 37-38; *Col. Laws N.Y.*, I, 519-21; *Minutes of the Common Council*, I, 134, 136-37, III, 277-78, IV, 447; *Cal.
Council Min.*, p. 435; Munsell, ed., *Annals of Albany*, VII, 174, VIII,
296; Fox, ed., *Minutes of the Court of Sessions*, pp. 66-67; Pelletreau,
ed., *Records of Smithtown*, p. 170.
[2] *Col. Laws N.Y.*, I, 617-18, 631, 762-64.

minor brawl among some slaves in Kingston was enough to get a rumor started that an uprising was in the making.[3] Whether founded or unfounded, however, anxiety over the possibility of insurrection was an unpleasant fact of life. It poisoned relations between the races and on two occasions threw the entire province into a deadly panic.

The principal danger of insurrection existed in New York City, where a large slave population had numerous opportunities for conspiracy. The slaves were able to meet daily at the wells and watering places of the town as they went about their regular tasks.[4] Lieutenant Governor Clarke expressed the concern felt by many whites that the slaves could thus meet "without the least molestation or interruption from the magistrates."[5] Moreover, the social climate of the town was conducive to conspiracy and subversion. The trade which had made New York a prosperous commercial center also lowered its moral tone. Privateers regularly passed through the port, and their carousals often made the town seem more like a pirate lair than the capital of a powerful province. With turbulent transients, too many disreputable taverns, and large numbers of Negro slaves, the town was a social powder keg.[6] That the situation might undermine the loyalty of the slaves and explode in insurrection kept the white inhabitants in a state of morbid anxiety.

The basis for such fears suddenly became real in 1712 when some slaves in New York City staged what turned out to be a badly executed but nevertheless bloody insurrection. The uprising was led by slaves

3 *New York Weekly Journal*, June 12, 1738.
4 De Voe, *The Market Book*, pp. 265-66.
5 *New York Weekly Journal*, August 9, 1742.
6 Henry Ingersoll, "The New York Plot of 1741," *The Green Bag*, XX (1908), 137-38.

from Africa who preferred death to permanent bondage. Preparations for the uprising were a well-kept secret, with recruits bound to silence by primitive but effective oaths.[7] Early in April, twenty-four of the conspirators met in an orchard on the northern outskirts of the town where muskets and other weapons had been cached. After arming themselves, they set fire to a nearby building and then took cover behind the trees. When the alarm was given and whites began to hurry toward the blaze, the slaves opened fire, killing five and wounding six. The whites who escaped the ambush returned to the town to arm themselves and alert the garrison. By the time the soldiers arrived, however, the townspeople had already counterattacked and driven the hopelessly outnumbered slaves into the woods.[8]

The uprising threw the town into a panic of preparation for what was feared would be a general insurrection. Every able-bodied man was put under arms and militia were brought in from nearby communities on Long Island. Governor Hunter ordered the arrest of any Negro traveling without a pass and urged the governors of Connecticut and Massachusetts to block the escape of rebels attempting to flee from New York.[9] It is doubtful whether any managed to escape, however, for cordons of militia tightly sealed off the rebels who had fled into the woods of northern Manhattan. The plight of these fugitives soon became desperate, for the woods offered neither shelter nor food. In the end, the principal leaders of the rebels committed suicide, and the rest, half-mad from hunger, surrendered. A total of seventy Negroes, counting those arrested outside New York City, were jailed within two weeks of the uprising.[10]

[7] Aptheker, *American Negro Slave Revolts*, p. 172.
[8] *Ibid.*
[9] Parish's Transcripts (1695-1713), p. 27.
[10] Valentine, *Manual* (1870), p. 766.

A special court convened by the governor made short work of the rebels. Of the twenty-seven slaves brought to trial for complicity in the plot, twenty-one were convicted and put to death.[11] Since the law authorized any degree of punishment in such cases, some unlucky slaves were executed with all the refinements of calculated barbarity. New Yorkers were treated to a round of grisly spectacles as Negroes were burned alive, racked and broken on the wheel, and gibbeted alive in chains.[12] In his report of the affair to England, Governor Hunter praised the judges for inventing "the most exemplary punishments that could be possibly thought of."[13] When put to the test, the ultimate support of the slave system was naked terror.

So great was the panic that slaves were arrested and convicted on the most specious sort of evidence.[14] Some slaves were denounced and prosecuted as a means of striking at their masters.[15] Governor Hunter, who intervened to save many Negroes who had been unjustly convicted, observed that there existed "no manner of convincing evidence against them, and nothing but the blind fury of a people much provoked could have condemned them."[16] By the end of the trials Hunter found that the prosecution of slaves had turned into "a party quarrel and the slaves fared just as the people stood affected to their masters."[17] If Hunter had not had the courage to correct these miscarriages of justice, the death toll among the slave population would have been greater. The atmosphere of unreasoning panic that pre-

11 Herbert Aptheker, *Essays in the History of the American Negro* (New York: International Publishers, 1945), p. 19.
12 Stokes, ed., *Iconography*, IV, 475.
13 Parish's Transcripts (1688-1760), pp. 15-16.
14 *Ibid.*
15 *N.Y. Col. Docs.*, V, 341-42, 357.
16 Parish's Transcripts (1688-1760), pp. 15-16.
17 *Cal. State Papers, Col.*, XXVI (1711-12), 307.

vailed caused one newspaper to compare the affair with the Salem witch trials.[18]

Nevertheless, that New York City had a close brush with disaster in the affair is undeniable. The conspirators were well organized and managed the difficult task of maintaining perfect security up to the very last moment. Only the ambush itself—a basically stupid strategy—saved the whites from a blood bath. If the rebels had struck directly at the sleeping town, drawing in others as they went, the uprising might have gained deadly momentum. Although the conspirators made a hopeless botch of things, they nevertheless gave the whites a shock from which they never fully recovered. The affair even had repercussions outside the province. Both Pennsylvania and Massachusetts halted the importation of slaves, the latter by outright prohibition and the former by a prohibitory import duty.[19]

The uprising resulted in an immediate tightening of the slave controls. For one thing, restrictions were imposed on the manumission of slaves. The presence of free Negroes was now cited as a hindrance to the effective regulation of the slaves, for freedmen were living examples that the Negro could aspire to something better than slavery. An attempt was therefore made to restrict the freedmen and, even more important, to keep their numbers from growing. In 1712 a statute was passed providing that in the future manumitted Negroes could not own houses or real property of any sort. Moreover, anyone wishing to manumit a slave was henceforth required to post a bond of £200.[20] The theory behind this legislation was that by discouraging manumission it would be possible to improve the effectiveness of the slave controls.

[18] *Boston News Letter*, April 14, 1712.
[19] Aptheker, *American Negro Slave Revolts*, p. 173.
[20] *Col. Laws N.Y.*, I, 764-65.

Anything that tended to alter the condition of the slave came under suspicion, and this included even the missionary efforts of the S.P.G. Elias Neau, the catechist for the Negroes of New York City, accused of abetting insurrection, was openly insulted on the streets. For a time it was not safe for him to appear in public.[21] The only basis for such charges was that two of his former students had been implicated, unjustly as it later turned out, in the plot.[22] Although the authorities cleared Neau of any wrongdoing, the missionary effort suffered a severe setback. In his report to the S.P.G. Neau observed that the uprising had convinced many slave-owners that any instruction—even religious instruction —"would be a means to make the slave more cunning and apter to wickedness."[23]

The events of 1712 greatly increased suspicion and set the stage for a bloody panic a generation later, when the slaves were suspected of conspiring to burn New York City and massacre the white population. The panic grew out of what was first regarded as an ordinary burglary committed late in February of 1741 at the shop of Robert Hogg, a well-known tobacconist. Hogg told the authorities that a few days before the crime a sailor named Christopher Wilson had been in the shop and had observed Mrs. Hogg while she was counting some gold coins. It soon came out that Wilson had a reputation for fraternizing with Negro slaves. When questioned, Wilson denied any knowledge of the crime but admitted having told two of his Negro friends about Hogg's gold. He also revealed that on the morning after the burglary he had visited a tavern kept by John Hughson and had seen his friends with a hatful of coins. This

---

21 Humphreys, *Account of the Endeavours by the S.P.G.*, pp. 9-10.
22 *Rev. and Misc. Papers*, III, 353.
23 Pierre, *Journal of Negro History*, I, 349-50.

was enough for the authorities, who promptly arrested the two Negroes and held them for the grand jury. Hughson was also detained briefly but was released when a search of the tavern failed to uncover anything incriminating.[24]

At this point an indentured servant of Hughson's named Mary Burton took a hand in the affair. While gossiping with the wife of one of the constables, Mary hinted that she knew something about the Hogg burglary. This brought her to the attention of the authorities and launched the series of disclosures which precipitated the panic. But these disclosures were not made immediately; rather, they were made only after Burton had mastered the knack of accusation. In the beginning her revelations were commonplace and most likely factual. She began by accusing Hughson, his wife, their daughter Sarah, and Peggy Kerry, a prostitute living at the tavern, of receiving stolen property from the slaves. She backed up her accusations by directing the constables to a cache of stolen goods buried under the tavern. Hughson was promptly arrested, and his wife, daughter, and Peggy Kerry were held as accomplices to the crime.[25]

While the investigation was still under way, a sudden rash of fires struck the town. As soon as one blaze was extinguished, another would break out somewhere else. The suddenness of the fires and the disappearance of goods from several of the burned buildings caused some to suspect arson.[26] But even more ominous from the standpoint of the whites was the growing insolence displayed by the slaves as the fires spread. The slaves

[24] Prince, "New York Plot of 1741," Typescript in coll. N.Y. Hist. Soc., p. 7.

[25] Daniel Horsmanden, *The New York Conspiracy: History of the Negro Plot, 1741-1742* (New York: Southwick & Pelsue, 1810), pp. 20-22.

[26] *Ibid.*, pp. 23-26.

were probably only enjoying the consternation of the whites, but the suspicion gradually took hold that they were setting the fires. This was seemingly confirmed when early in March a slave was caught looting a burning building.[27] So convinced were the townspeople that arsonists were at work that the city council offered a reward of £100 "for the discovery of the villainous conspiracy."[28]

With rumors flying in every direction, the town was plagued with fear when Mary Burton finally appeared before the grand jury to testify about the Hogg burglary. Interest in the crime had by now been overshadowed by the fires, so most New Yorkers paid little attention to her first appearance. Their attitude soon changed, however, when Burton hinted that she knew something about the fires. After a show of some hesitation which the judges easily overcame, she told the grand jury that the fires had been set by slaves on orders from Hughson. In a rambling, confused tale she accused the Hughsons, Peggy Kerry, and two slaves named Quack and Cuffee of plotting to burn the city and massacre the whites. After the slaughter, Hughson was to be proclaimed king, and any white women who survived the massacre were to be divided among the slaves.[29]

Quack and Cuffee were the first to be tried on the basis of Burton's sensational accusations. What happened to them was of crucial importance, for the later prosecution of both whites and Negroes hinged largely on precedents set at their trial. And the worst precedent of all was set by the lawyers of the city, who refused to a man to assist in the defense.[30] This boycott not only

27 *New York Weekly Journal,* April 27, 1741.
28 *Minutes of the Common Council,* V, 17-18.
29 Horsmanden, *The New York Conspiracy,* pp. 37-40.
30 Valentine, *Manual* (1856), pp. 448-50.

crippled the defense but encouraged the prosecutor, Attorney General Bradley, to use tactics which the mere presence of a defense counsel would surely have prevented. To corroborate Burton's story, Bradley used a convicted thief named Arthur Price to spy on the defendants in prison while they were awaiting trial. Thus Price was able to testify that both Quack and Cuffee had admitted to him that they had set several fires on orders from Hughson.[31] The defendants, on the other hand, insisted that Price was lying, that no admissions had been made, and that they were innocent of any wrongdoing. Notwithstanding the testimony of their masters, who swore under oath that both slaves were at home when the alleged arsons occurred, Quack and Cuffee were found guilty on all counts and sentenced to be burned at the stake.[32]

The executions were not carried out immediately, however, for the authorities were more interested in smashing what seemed to be a dangerous conspiracy than in executing individual conspirators. Although offers of clemency were made to Quack and Cuffee for the purpose of eliciting information, both slaves steadfastly asserted their innocence. Only at the very end when they were brought to the execution ground did their nerve fail them. Terrified by the sight of the stake and the wood piled high for their incineration, they broke down and gave depositions naming Hughson as "the first contriver of the plot."[33] But the confessions came too late to save them, for the crowd which had turned out for the spectacle became unruly when the sheriff attempted to return them to jail. Not wanting a riot, the

---

[31] Horsmanden, *The New York Conspiracy*, pp. 60-62.
[32] *Ibid.*, pp. 79-96.
[33] Valentine, *Manual* (1866), pp. 816-17.

129

sheriff decided to give the people what they had come to see and so went through with the executions.[34]

By the time the Hughsons and Peggy Kerry came to trial, their fate was not really in doubt. Mary Burton told her now familiar story, and Arthur Price, repeating his prior performance, testified that Peggy and Mrs. Hughson had confessed their guilt to him in prison.[35] Price of course had no real standing as a witness, for convicted felons were not legally qualified to testify against anyone. For the prosecutor to use such evidence was bad enough, but what followed was even worse. Bradley then called several white witnesses who testified about the depositions given by Quack and Cuffee. These depositions were not admissible directly, for slaves were barred by statute from testifying against whites.[36] And testimony about the depositions was also inadmissible under the hearsay rule. But the legally un- schooled defendants had no way of knowing what was admissible and failed to object to the damaging testi- mony. Their utter helplessness in coping with Bradley's tricks made the outcome clearly predictable. They were all found guilty and sentenced to be hanged. Hughson, his wife, and Peggy Kerry were executed within the week. Sarah Hughson, however, was granted a reprieve so that the authorities might try to persuade her to co- operate in the investigation.[37]

In the beginning most of Burton's accusations were directed against Negro bondsmen. Since the Hughsons and Peggy Kerry had already been jailed for receiving stolen property, she ran no real risk in linking them to the conspiracy. But as the trials progressed, Burton

34 Horsmanden, *The New York Conspiracy*, pp. 96-102.
35 *Ibid.*, pp. 109-20.
36 *Col. Laws N.Y.*, I, 597-98.
37 Horsmanden, *The New York Conspiracy*, pp. 109-20, 122-40.

became more and more aware of her deadly power. To her amazement the hitherto obscure drudge found the authorities hanging on her every word, indicting and prosecuting whoever was mentioned in her increasingly wild and lurid testimony. Emboldened by success, she began hurling accusations in every direction, denouncing whites and Negroes alike. And the accused in turn became accusers in order to obtain the pardon offered to those who cooperated in the investigation. Thus accusation fed upon accusation until it seemed that most of the slaves and many of the whites were involved in the plot.[38]

This epidemic of mutual incrimination soon filled the jails, compelling the authorities to suspend the circuit courts for the rest of the year.[39] But even more important, it slowed down the prosecution. With accusations flying in every direction, the attorney general had to unravel a mass of wildly conflicting allegations. The result was a respite for the accused and an opportunity for the community to regain some sense of balance. As the jails filled and confessions multiplied, anxieties subsided and life gradually returned to normal. Although the confessions gave the conspiracy enormous scope, they paradoxically provided a measure of psychological relief. With the accused confessing in droves, there was every reason to regard the conspiracy as smashed and the worst over.[40]

That the panic did not subside completely can be traced to the untimely intervention of Governor Oglethorpe of Georgia. For years Oglethorpe had been harassed by Spaniards from Florida who crossed the frontier to incite the Indians and slaves of Georgia to revolt.

38 Valentine, *Manual* (1856), pp. 448-50.
39 *Cal. Council Min.,* p. 338.
40 *New York Weekly Journal,* July 27, 1741.

Driven to distraction by these forays, he came to regard them as part of a larger plot against all the English colonies. The outbreak of war with Spain in 1739 and the failure of his own expedition against St. Augustine the following year plunged this moody man into the deepest despair. Convinced that his own and other colonies were in deadly peril, he bombarded officials everywhere with letters warning them against Spanish plots. One of the letters which he sent in 1741 warned Lieutenant Governor Clarke that the Spaniards would probably attempt to burn New York City. Citing his own troubles in Georgia, he warned that Catholic priests were likely to be sent into New York by Spain to organize the destruction of the port.[41]

Oglethorpe's letter not only revived the conspiracy scare but gave it much more sinister dimensions. It also released long-standing religious animosities. Catholics were detested in the English colonies, not only on religious grounds but especially for their known adherence to the Stuart pretenders. It was a capital offense in New York for a Catholic priest even to enter the province.[42] And the warning certainly seemed plausible in the light of past experience. The Spaniards had a well-earned reputation for plotting and had in fact used priests to subvert the slaves of the border colonies. Already unnerved by their own brush with incendiarism, many New Yorkers confused plausibility with probability and took Oglethorpe's warning at face value.[43]

In any event, the letter inspired a spate of rumors that the province was being infiltrated by Spanish agents. New Yorkers now recalled the strange case of

[41] Valentine, *Manual* (1856), p. 769. See Smith, *History of the Late Province of New York*, II, 60.

[42] Aptheker, *American Negro Slave Revolts*, p. 195.

[43] Joseph C. Carroll, *Slave Insurrections in the United States, 1800-1865* (Boston: Chapman & Grimes, 1938), pp. 122-23.

Luke Barrington, who about five years before had caused a minor uproar in Ulster County. Barrington, a schoolmaster, not only consorted with Irish Catholic servants but publicly toasted the health of the king of Spain. The latter imprudence soon landed him in jail, from which he subsequently escaped and disappeared from the province.[44] The Barrington case had long been regarded as something of a mystery, though hardly a sinister one. The Oglethorpe letter now put the affair in an entirely different light. It convinced contemporaries that Barrington had been a Spanish agent and that Spain was behind the recent Negro plot.[45]

The subsequent hunt for Spanish agents resulted in the arrest of a schoolmaster named John Ury. Ury, who had arrived in New York City a few months before the fires had begun, claimed to be a non-juring clergyman of the Church of England, but was suspected of being a Catholic priest. The suspicion sprang mainly from Ury's skill as a Latinist and his penchant for theological disputation. Most New Yorkers had highly stylized ideas of how to detect Catholic priests. Unfortunately for Ury, Latin and religious casuistry were important elements of the stereotype. Thus he became the focal point of all the suspicions stirred up by Oglethorpe's letter. It was left to Mary Burton, however, to bring about his arrest by denouncing him as a Catholic priest and the real leader of the Negro conspiracy.[46]

The case against Ury was extremely weak, even by the loose standards of the other conspiracy trials. For one thing, Burton's new accusations could not be reconciled with her earlier testimony against Hughson. In all her testimony she had named Hughson as the chief con-

<hr>

44 *Colden Papers,* VIII, 228-89.
45 *Ibid.*
46 Valentine, *Manual* (1870), p. 770.

spirator; she made no charges at all against Ury, nor did she say anything to indicate that the alleged plot had religious or political implications. Only after Oglethorpe's letter had brought Ury under suspicion did Burton belatedly remember that he was the real leader of the plot. But her story was now so riddled with inconsistencies that some observers began to doubt her credibility.[47]

Attorney General Bradley, however, had no doubts. Ignoring the contradictions in Burton's story, he set out to corroborate her new allegations. Every device that guile and shabby maneuver could muster was employed to frame a case against Ury. Bradley decided that the time had come to make use of Sarah Hughson, who had been languishing in prison since the execution of her parents. He promised her a pardon if she would corroborate Burton's story and warned that she would be executed if she refused. Having lived for months in the shadow of the gallows, the terrified girl grasped at the offer and agreed to testify against Ury.[48]

Bradley began his case against Ury with a furious tirade against Catholics and the Spanish Inquisition. With little real evidence to offer the jury, he sought to muddy the waters at the outset by appealing to religious prejudice. Then he called Mary Burton, who identified Ury as the chief conspirator. She also accused Ury of performing Catholic rites which were attended by the conspirators at Hughson's tavern.[49] Burton's testimony of course was damaging, but it also gave the defense a priceless opportunity to exploit its contradictions. A skillful cross-examination would have impeached the

[47] *Ibid.*
[48] Horsmanden, *The New York Conspiracy*, pp. 138, 162, 183, 223, 246.
[49] *Ibid.*, p. 292.

witness and thereby demolished the prosecution's case. But Ury was not skillful. He asked Burton a few inconsequential questions which did not even touch the issue of inconsistency.[50] This is most surprising, for Ury was an intelligent man—better educated and far cleverer than anyone yet tried. Perhaps he was simply unfamiliar with the testimony given at the Hughson trial and therefore unaware that contradictions existed. In any event, he failed to attack where Burton was clearly vulnerable and thereby missed his best chance of saving himself.

Bradley then called his corroborating witnesses. The first was a soldier named William Kane, who had also been accused by Burton. In order to save himself, Kane agreed to cooperate with the prosecution. He told a wild story of being admitted to the conspiracy by Hughson and Ury in the presence of a group of Negro slaves. He also accused Ury of performing a Catholic ritual which was intended to bind the conspirators together.[51] Bradley's second corroborating witness was Sarah Hughson, who testified that everything Burton had said was true.[52] She was half-hysterical by now and only answered in the affirmative to the leading questions asked by Bradley. When she had finished, Bradley read Oglethorpe's letter to the jury and rested his case.[53]

Ury's defense was much better than his inept cross-examination of Mary Burton would have led one to expect. It was intelligent, well reasoned, and, under normal circumstances, probably would have been sufficient to clear him. He called several character witnesses who testified that his personal life was blameless and

[50] Valentine, *Manual* (1870), p. 770.
[51] Horsmanden, *The New York Conspiracy*, p. 295.
[52] *Ibid.*
[53] Valentine, *Manual* (1870), p. 770.

135

that there was nothing at all to support the rumor that he was a Catholic priest. Other witnesses accounted for his whereabouts at the times when he was alleged to have been at Hughson's performing rituals for groups of conspirators. In a moving summation that was eloquent and restrained, he told the court that he was innocent and rebuked Bradley for attempting to prejudice the jury against him. But he spoke in vain, for it took the jury only fifteen minutes to bring in a verdict of guilty.[54]

The execution of Ury marked the end of the conspiracy panic. Slaves continued to be arrested, but tensions eased and the townspeople gradually regained their equilibrium. And as life again returned to normal, many New Yorkers began to have second thoughts about the whole affair. Some were openly critical, especially the slaveholders who had lost valuable bondsmen. Altogether, fourteen slaves had been burned at the stake, eighteen hanged, and seventy-two deported from the province. Another fifty were in jail awaiting trial and therefore of no possible use to their masters.[55] These were the slaveowners who took the lead in demanding a halt to the hunt for conspirators. Judge Horsmanden, who presided over the trials, noted that the masters closed ranks against the investigation "when it comes home to their own houses and is like to affect their own properties in Negroes."[56]

But soon Horsmanden too had reason to take another view when the affair suddenly took an unexpected turn. Intoxicated with self-importance, Mary Burton denounced several prominent whites to the grand jury. Attorney General Bradley, who had hitherto

54 *Colden Papers*, II, 225.
55 Parish's Transcripts (1729-60), p. 34.
56 *Colden Papers*, II, 226.

accepted everything she had said, was stunned by the new accusations.[57] Not only was his star witness lying, but she was lying so crudely that even the dullest dolt could see through her perjury. Even Horsmanden, whose credulity was boundless where Burton was concerned, was forced to admit that her allegations "staggered one's belief."[58] Exactly what she said is unknown, for Horsmanden suppressed the grand jury minutes in order to protect the credibility of her previous testimony.[59]

With Burton completely out of control, the authorities had no choice but to drop the affair if they were to save their own reputations. If the trials had continued and Burton kept talking, a public reaction against those responsible for the prior prosecutions and miscarriage of justice would have been inevitable. The authorities therefore beat a hasty retreat while there was still time. Even Horsmanden, who was by far the most vociferous defender of the proceedings, urged "a little relaxation from this intricate pursuit."[60] Thus the "intricate pursuit" ground to a halt, ironically on the same note as it had begun—the perjury of Mary Burton. The ruthless lying which had caused so much injustice in the end halted the injustice.

It was perhaps inevitable that such an affair should end on a note of deceit and obfuscation. The authorities simply could not admit that they had presided over a bloody hoax. The death toll had been too great for them to admit that they had been hoodwinked. They had no choice but to nurture the fiction that the proceedings had run an orderly course. The provincial council did its part by designating a day of thanksgiving

57 *Ibid.*, II, 227.
58 *Ibid.*
59 Valentine, *Manual* (1870), p. 770.
60 *Colden Papers*, II, 227.

"for deliverance from the conspiracy."[61] And when Burton claimed the reward for exposing the plot, the New York City officials who had accepted her every utterance had no choice but to pay. Thus Burton got not only her money but also a self-serving vote of thanks from the city council "for the great service she has done."[62] To the relief of practically everyone, she thereupon disappeared from the province.[63]

Mary Burton played a deadly role in the conspiracy panic. She did in New York what Titus Oates had done earlier in England, and the Parris girls in Massachusetts. But the community as a whole was also responsible, for it used the conspiracy trials as a vent for its own prejudice and insecurity. Burton was an ignorant drudge whose slovenly lies would have collapsed in a moment if the authorities had been seriously interested in getting at the truth. But what the community wanted was not truth but a release from fear. The refusal of the entire New York bar to defend any of the accused is the best gauge of what the community really wanted. Burton was not alone to blame, for the authorities consciously encouraged her perjury. In the beginning at least, she testified haltingly, fabricating her story out of hints and leading questions from the attorney general and the judges. Certainly she was a contemptible liar, but those who abetted her accusations were willing accomplices.[64]

From a legal standpoint, the conspiracy trials were judicial murders. Except for the testimony given by Mary Burton and William Kane, all the evidence offered by the prosecution was legally inadmissible for one reason or another. Neither Arthur Price nor Sarah

61 *Cal. Council Min.*, p. 338.
62 Parish's Transcripts (1740-47), p. 10.
63 *Ibid.*, pp. 18-19.
64 Prince, "New York Plot of 1741," Typescript in coll. N.Y. Hist. Soc., pp. 12-13.

Hughson was a qualified witness, for in colonial times the courts excluded the testimony of convicted felons. And the testimony given on the depositions of Quack and Cuffee violated the rule against hearsay. If the inadmissible evidence had been properly challenged, the prosecution would have had no case. But because the defendants had to stand trial without counsel, most of these defects went unchallenged. And when Ury, who was more knowledgeable than the rest, had the presence of mind to challenge Sarah Hughson's standing as a witness, Bradley hastily procured a pardon to remove her felon's disability.[65] By such unconscionable intrigues and shabby maneuvers were the defendants sent to the gallows.

Only two other slave conspiracies were uncovered in New York in the eighteenth century and neither of these affected New York City. The first involved about thirteen slaves in Schenectady who in 1761 formed a plot to burn and loot the town. In many ways the plot paralleled the New York City plot of 1741, though no fires were actually set. The conspiracy was discovered when some of the plotters were overheard in a tavern as they talked about their plans. Three were arrested, but the rest managed to escape to Canada.[66] The other conspiracy, uncovered in Ulster County in 1775, posed no real threat to the whites. Its object was simply a mass break for freedom to Canada. Twenty slaves were arrested for complicity in the plot, but the authorities were convinced that at least twice that number were involved.[67]

Although New York did not have to contend with many organized slave plots, the few that were uncovered

65 Horsmanden, *The New York Conspiracy*, p. 295.
66 *New York Weekly Post-Boy*, August 13, 1761.
67 *New York Mercury*, March 6, 1775.

left the province badly shaken. The conspiracy scare of 1741, for example, left scars that never really healed. Reflecting on the affair, one contemporary observed that anyone who purchased slaves after that experience would "have only himself to blame for the consequences."[68] Though stricter laws were passed to reduce the number of disorderly taverns and tighten enforcement of the curfew, many whites lost confidence in the effectiveness of any slave controls.[69] The events of 1741 seemed to demonstrate that even the strictest preventive measures could not keep the slaves from plotting. Even outside New York City any sign of slave unrest was thereafter sufficient to drive the whites to extremes. During the summer of 1741, for example, a slave was hanged at Kingston for assault, a crime ordinarily not punishable by death.[70] The plot convinced most New Yorkers that the slaves spent virtually all their free time planning the destruction of the whites. A residue of anxiety remained as a reminder to the masters that slavery for the Negro meant fear and insecurity for the whites. It was a toll the whites would have to pay as long as slavery existed.

[68] *Colden Papers*, II, 253.
[69] *New York Weekly Journal*, August 9, 1742.
[70] Justices Court, Ulster County, Kingston, July 1, 1741, Hist. Docs. Coll., Klapper Library, Queens College.

VIII. MANUMISSION
AND ANTISLAVERY

"A DESIRE OF OBTAINING FREEDOM . . . UN-
HAPPILY REIGNS THROUGHOUT THE GENERAL-
ITY OF SLAVES AT PRESENT."
—*New York Weekly Mercury, November 27, 1780.*

M ASTERS frequently took advantage of the
desire of slaves for freedom to provide an incentive to
loyal service. Private emancipation always played an important role in making slavery an efficient system of
labor. Slaves were freed both as a reward for past services and in some cases as an inducement to loyal service
in the future. Aggressive slaves often compelled their
owners to enter into manumission agreements by deliberately neglecting their duties.[1] Indeed, given the character of the typical New York slave—his intelligence
and range of skills—it is doubtful whether the slave system could have functioned efficiently in any other way.
Some contemporaries regarded the slave's hope of gaining freedom within the system as the best possible defense against insurrection. Governor Hunter, who
shared this view, repeatedly supported measures designed to encourage slaveowners to use manumission as
a reward for faithful service.[2]

For many years there were virtually no restrictions
on the master's right to free his slaves. Since the slaves
were legally chattels, the slaveowner had the power to

1 Register of Manumissions, pp. 65, 66, 73.
2 *Cal. State Papers, Col.*, XXVIII (1714-15), 338.

141

dispose of them in any way he saw fit, and this included the power to renounce his rights of ownership completely. Ordinarily the courts interfered only if the owner manumitted a slave in order to avoid the claims of creditors. Until the eighteenth century the legal regulation of manumission varied considerably from town to town. But the crux of all the regulations was that masters might not abandon aged or infirm slaves under the pretext of freeing them. Since the local overseers of the poor were responsible for indigent freedmen, in most places the masters were required to obtain their approval before freeing a slave. Some towns insisted upon a manumission bond to guarantee that the freedman would not become a public charge.[3]

Emancipation came under provincial control for the first time in 1712 as a result of the uprising at New York City. The Assembly passed a law requiring slave-owners to post a bond of £200 to guarantee that their freedmen were capable of self-support. Slaves manumitted by will were to be bonded in the same amount by the executor of the estate or the manumission would be void.[4] The real purpose of the law was not to keep freedmen off the public dole but to discourage manumission by making it financially prohibitive. The uprising convinced the lawmakers that free Negroes exerted a bad influence on the slave force and that the safest course was to make slavery prescriptive.[5] Since few masters were willing to post a bond of £200, the law virtually ended private emancipation.

This restriction of manumission was soon recognized for what it was: a misconceived policy which stirred up rather than prevented slave discontent. The

3 Cobb, *Inquiry into the Law of Slavery*, pp. 279-83, 294.
4 *Col. Laws N.Y.*, I, 764-65.
5 *Ibid.*, I, 761.

restriction removed the one incentive that slaves had to render loyal service and inevitably brought about a slump in slave morale. Governor Hunter warned the Assembly that the virtual ban on manumission was unjust and would in fact increase the danger of insurrection.[6] He pointed to the case of a much-respected slave in New York City who had been deprived of his freedom under the law. The slave had been manumitted by will, and since he had helped his master build up a considerable fortune, he received a bequest of money and a slave so that he might carry on the master's business for himself. The executor, however, refused to post the statutory bond, so the Negro lost both his freedom and the legacy. Occurrences like this, said Hunter, were not likely to promote loyalty among the slaves.[7]

Most slaveholders agreed that the manumission restriction served neither their interests nor the interests of the community. Hostility to the law was so widespread that in 1717 the Assembly voted for repeal and enacted a substitute measure which required manumitting owners to post only a nominal bond that their freedmen would not become a public charge.[8] Moreover, the law allowed the local authorities to waive the bond entirely if they were satisfied that the slave was capable of self-support.[9] In some counties the overseers of the poor accepted personal sureties in lieu of the bond. It was enough for the surety to give his guarantee that the freedman "shall not be a charge to any town in this province."[10]

6 *Cal. State Papers, Col.*, XXVIII (1714-15), 338.
7 *N.Y. Col. Docs.*, V, 461.
8 *Col. Laws N.Y.*, I, 922.
9 Kingston Records, Manumissions, Hist. Docs. Coll., Klapper Library, Queens College.
10 Court of General Sessions of the Peace, Ulster County, Kingston, November 4, 1740, May 1, 1750, Hist. Docs. Coll., Klapper Library, Queens College.

To make certain that their freedmen never became a public charge, manumitting masters often required newly freed slaves to provide against old age and indigence. One master on Long Island set up a private system of social security for his freedmen, who were obliged to pay part of their earnings into a fund to tide them over hard times.[11] A similar plan was set up in Flushing by a farmer named James Thorne, who required all his freedmen to contribute £3 annually into a fund to provide for their old age.[12] Another master in Scarsdale manumitted several slaves in his will "on condition that they pay to my executors forty shillings, which sum my executors are to put to interest for their support at any time when thought necessary."[13] Such arrangements served the interests of both masters and slaves. The slave obtained freedom with some measure of security against old age and indigence while the master was relieved of the burden of supporting freedmen who fell upon hard times after manumission.

When a very young slave was manumitted by will, the emancipation usually became effective as soon as he was old enough to be self-supporting. Unless slave children were bequeathed directly to their parents, the master would make special provisions for their support and education with a view to preparing them for freedom. Testators usually entrusted young slaves to a guardian who would be responsible for teaching them a trade. One master in Scarsdale left detailed instructions for the education of several children emancipated under his will.[14] Another master in New York City bequeathed £25 to purchase tools for the use of his young freedman

11 *Abstracts of Wills*, XII, 290-92.
12 *Ibid.*, XII, 374-75.
13 *Ibid.*, XIII, 354-57.
14 William S. Pelletreau, ed., *Early Wills of Westchester County* (New York: Francis P. Harper, 1898), p. 179.

in learning a trade.[15] David Hunter, a Westchester farmer, directed his heirs to educate several "little Negroes and bring them up to a good business."[16] As soon as they became self-supporting, such slaves were given certificates of manumission.

Most manumissions were motivated not by philanthropy but by pressures applied by the slaves themselves. Some bondsmen persuaded their masters to enter into agreements giving them freedom in return for a stipulated term of faithful service. Others won the opportunity to buy their way to freedom by working nights or hiring their own time.[17] Because many masters were willing to accept payment in installments, slaves often earned their way to freedom gradually over a period of time. Skilled slaves sometimes convinced uncooperative masters of the wisdom of entering into such agreements by malingering until they got what they wanted. In most cases, however, this was unnecessary, for it was generally recognized that the productivity of slaves had a direct relation to the expectation of freedom.[18]

From a legal standpoint, the effectiveness of a manumission agreement depended on a number of technicalities which probably had nothing to do with the real intent of either of the parties. Where the agreement was executory in form, that is, to take effect at a future time, no promise of freedom, whether oral or written, could be enforced against the master. Such agreements were legally ineffectual for lack of consideration. Because both the money and labor of the slave already belonged to the master, neither could be used to

15 *Abstracts of Wills,* VII, 178-80.
16 *Ibid.,* VIII, 322-23.
17 Register of Manumissions, *passim; Jamaica Town Records,* III, 346-47, 349-55; *Abstracts of Wills,* XV, 114-16.
18 *Cal. State Papers, Col.,* XXVIII (1714-15), 338.

support a claim to freedom.[19] Indeed, the law did not even allow the slave to testify in his own behalf in a suit to enforce the agreement.[20] On the other hand, a post-dated deed of emancipation actually delivered to the slave was effectual because nothing more remained to be done by the master. Delivery of the deed gave the slave freedom subject to defeasance only for failure to comply with its conditions. The burden of enforcement in this case was on the master, so the slave was fully protected.[21]

The courts applied the same test to testamentary emancipations. Where the manumission was executory in form, the slave obtained no rights which were enforceable against the master. Revocation of the emancipating clause nullified the manumission even though the slave had already performed his part of the bargain. Likewise, if the master sold the slave, the sale revoked the emancipation and the slave remained in permanent bondage.[22] But a deed of emancipation to take effect at the master's death and actually delivered to the slave was irrevocable. The subsequent sale of the slave did not impair the deed, and at the original seller's death the slave automatically became free. All that the buyers of such a slave obtained was the right to his labor during the lifetime of the manumitting owner.[23]

A testamentary emancipation was binding on the testator's estate regardless of the desires of the executor and heirs. If the executor sold the slave instead of issuing a deed of emancipation as directed by the will, the

19 *Smith v. Hoff,* 1 Cowen's New York Reports 127 (New York Supreme Court, 1823).

20 *Col. Laws N.Y.,* I, 597-98.

21 *Kettletas v. Fleet,* 1 Anthon's Nisi Prius Reports 36 (New York, 1808).

22 *In re Michel,* 14 Johnson's Reports 324 (New York Supreme Court, 1817).

23 *In re Tom,* 5 Johnson's Reports 365 (New York Supreme Court, 1810).

slave could obtain his freedom against any purchaser. The courts construed the will as sufficient notice to prospective buyers that the slave was not vendible.[24] Any attempt by executors or heirs to deprive the slave of his freedom was bound to outrage public opinion. In 1763, when the heirs of Isaac Johnson attempted to sell a young slave manumitted by Johnson's will, a committee of whites quickly formed to protect the slave. The heirs and public were put on notice that any attempt to deprive the slave of his freedom would result in prosecution of the culprits. In this case the warning alone was sufficient to obtain the slave's release.[25]

Some emancipations of course were motivated by a moral revulsion against slavery. One master in Westchester County manumitted his slaves "believing it to be consistent with the will of kind Providence, who hath created all nations with one blood."[26] Numerous deeds of emancipation were recorded wherein the masters explained that they were freeing their slaves "in order to serve the cause of humanity."[27] Likewise, manumitting owners often attempted to provide for their slaves after emancipation.[28] Petrus Smedes of Kingston left detailed instructions in his will for the care of his freedmen. One of his ex-slaves was to be provided with "three shirts, one pair of moccasins, three pair stockings, two linen breeches, two pair shoes yearly, one waistcoat and one jacket every two years, and one great coat every three years."[29] A master on Long Island set aside a tract of

24 Cobb, *Inquiry into the Law of Slavery*, pp. 298-99.
25 *New York Mercury*, July 18, 1763.
26 *Abstracts of Wills*, X, 8.
27 Register of Manumissions, pp. 63, 65, 66, *et seq.*
28 *Abstracts of Wills*, V, 61-62, 113-14, 165-66; VI, 165-66, 275, 417; VII, 34-36, 147-48, 266, 346-47; VIII, 32, 243-45; IX, 84, 118-19; X, 92-93; XI, 86-87; XII, 147-48, 191-93, 241-42; XIII, 304-6, 357-59; XIV, 102-3, 136-38, 202-7, 210-11, 236, 316-17; XV, 15, 32-35, 53-56, 96-97, 109-12, 128-30, 143-45, 220-23, 231-34.
29 *Ibid.*, XII, 147-48.

land for the benefit of his ex-slaves.[30] Another master in Westchester bequeathed an annuity to be used to assist his aged and infirm freedmen.[31] These expressions of concern were reminders that some masters regarded the slaves as more than chattels.

Nevertheless, masters often practiced a selective type of philanthropy which ignored the moral aspects of slavery and thereby rendered their own actions equivocal. In most cases one or two slaves were singled out for special consideration, and the favored ones were usually chosen as a reward for faithful service.[32] One master in New York City sent five bondsmen to Virginia in the same year that he freed a favorite slave.[33] Another master in Westchester manumitted three of his four slaves by will while leaving instructions that the fourth, "having behaved contrary to the rule of a good servant," was to be sold.[34] It is clear that many slaves who received seemingly gratuitous manumissions earned the right to be free fully as much as those who bargained directly for freedom. Often the only difference between the philanthropic manumission and the earned manumission was that the latter made the price of freedom explicit.

Even testators frequently exacted a price for freedom by requiring slaves to pay an income to beneficiaries of the estate as a condition of emancipation.[35] Failure to pay automatically revoked the manumission and returned the freedman to slavery. A Long Island owner agreed to emancipate a slave "provided he will

---

30 *Ibid.*, X, 92-93.
31 *Ibid.*, XII, 247-49; XIII, 357-59.
32 *Ibid.*, V, 126-28; VI, 1, 350-51, 406-7; VIII, 63-64; IX, 103-4, 135-36; XII, 3, 147-48, 182-83, 241-42, 290-92; XIV, 175-76; XV, 104-6, 128-30.
33 *Ibid.*, IX, 103-4.
34 *Ibid.*, XII, 182-83
35 *Ibid.*, V, 74, 149-50; X, 67; XII, 374; XIV, 202-7; XV, 77-78.

return to my executors yearly the sum of £3 for the use of my wife and children."[36] Another master in Hempstead agreed to emancipate a slave "if he can pay my son or his heirs the sum of £4 per year for eighteen years."[37] Such manumissions can hardly be considered philanthropic, for they gave the slave nothing but the chance to earn his own freedom.

Slaves were invariably eager to obtain freedom regardless of the conditions imposed. No record exists of a slave's ever opting for bondage under any circumstances. After buying their own freedom, some worked hard to buy relatives and friends out of slavery.[38] That they dearly prized freedom can be seen in numerous legal actions brought against whites who attempted to enslave them.[39] One free Negro who had been working at hire won a suit against an employer who falsely claimed him as a slave.[40] In another case several Negroes won their freedom from sharpers who sought to enslave them for non-existent debts.[41] Some freedmen not only regained their liberty through the courts but recovered compensation for unlawful detention.[42]

The Quakers were for many years the only organized opponents of slavery. Indeed, much of the unpopularity of the Quakers in colonial times can be traced to their uncompromising hostility to slavery.[43] As early as 1718 a Quaker pamphleteer named John Burling urged

36 *Ibid.*, X, 271-72.
37 *Ibid.*, X, 63-64.
38 Register of Manumissions, pp. 65, 66, 73.
39 Minutes of the New York Manumission Society, March 21, 1797, MS. coll. N.Y. Hist. Soc.
40 *Ibid.*, June 20, 1794.
41 *Ibid.*
42 *Ibid.*, April 16, 1795.
43 Carter G. Woodson, *The Education of the Negro prior to 1861* (New York: G. P. Putnam's Sons, 1915), pp. 43-45.

the Quakers of Long Island to free any slaves who came into their possession.[44] In 1767 the Quaker congregation of Flushing formally condemned slavery as incompatible with the principles of Christianity.[45] In 1771 the Quakers adopted an antislavery resolution at their annual provincial convention. The resolution was to be implemented on the local level by Quaker freedom committees which were to urge individual slaveholders to manumit their bondsmen as a religious duty.[46] Quakers who refused to comply were ousted from their local congregations.[47] So rapid was the progress of antislavery among the Quakers that the statutory restrictions on emancipation were often disregarded. Because Quakers often neglected to record their emancipations as the law required, many slaves received defective manumissions—"Quaker freedom" as it was called. To protect these freedmen, the legislature finally enacted a law validating such emancipations retroactively.[48]

Many non-Quakers were also opposed to slavery, though for somewhat different reasons. Whatever objections others had to the slave system did not stem from moral considerations but from fear for their own safety. Shortly after the uprising of 1712 Governor Hunter urged the legislature to encourage the importation of indentured servants as a substitute for slave labor.[49] And Governor Cosby was so disturbed about the risks of slavery that he warned against "the disadvantages that at-

44 Esther Copley, *A History of Slavery and Its Abolition* (London: Houlston & Stoneman, 1839), pp. 179-85.
45 Scharf, *History of Westchester County*, I, 30.
46 Leo Hirsch, "The Negro and New York, 1783-1865," *The Journal of Negro History*, XVI (1931), 385.
47 Baird, *History of Rye*, p. 188.
48 *Laws of New York, 1798*, XXVII.
49 *Journal of the Legislative Council of the Colony of New York* (Albany: T. Weed, 1861), I, 333.

tend the too great importation of Negroes."[50] Cosby predicted that the province could expect serious trouble if the Negro population continued to grow. On this much at least, Cosby and his journalistic critic John Peter Zenger were in complete agreement. In 1737 Zenger printed an editorial which urged the Assembly to enact slave tariffs high enough to stem the influx of slaves and provide a subsidy for the importation of white servants.[51]

Antislavery first became a political issue in the course of the emerging conflict between the colonies and England in the 1760's. The assertion of the natural rights doctrine by American polemicists helped to alter the general conception of the Negro and slavery. White Americans demanding political freedom for themselves found it difficult to justify continued slavery for the Negro.[52] And for the most part they did not try, not even in the plantation colonies, where the slave system was deeply entrenched in the social system. In every colony slavery came under scathing attack as a violation of natural rights. New York newspapers denounced slaveholding and reported incidents underscoring the basic brutality of the system. Although most of the incidents reported occurred in the West Indies, where conditions had no parallel in New York, such reports fed the antislavery impulse.[53] One New York City newspaper printed an editorial describing the Negro bondsmen as "poor pagans whom Christians have thought fit to consider cattle."[54]

50 Smith, *History of the Late Province of New York*, II, 11-12.
51 *New York Weekly Journal*, March 28, 1737.
52 John W. Cromwell, *The Negro in American History* (Washington: The American Negro Academy, 1914), p. 10; James Z. George, *Political History of Slavery in the United States* (New York: The Neale Publishing Co., 1915), pp. 9-10.
53 *New York Pacquet*, July 11, 1763.
54 *New York Weekly Post-Boy*, March 24, 1760.

151

The newspapers also published attacks on slavery by English abolitionists. These polemics were often coupled with stories about Negroes who had performed heroic acts or who had in some way distinguished themselves.[55] Such stories improved the image of the Negro and thereby underscored his right to freedom. In a stinging attack on slavery one newspaper printed a supposed dialogue between an Englishman and a Negro slave: "What you think massa Inglis," asks the slave, "if black man come steal you, steal wife, and take them quite away, where no see one another again?"[56] For Americans proclaiming the doctrine of natural rights, such a question stung the conscience.

The Revolution intensified the opposition to slavery. Abolitionists such as John Woolman and Nathaniel Appleton spoke out to remind Americans that slavery was incompatible with their own claims to freedom.[57] In 1774 the distillers of New York City made their position clear by unanimously voting not to distill molasses or syrup intended for the slave trade.[58] So general was the ideological reaction that slavery was condemned by almost all the leaders of the Revolution. Washington, Jefferson, and Madison, slaveholders all, made statements supporting the principle of gradual abolition. Jefferson's first draft of the Declaration of Independence contained a sweeping condemnation of the slave trade and England's refusal to allow legislation "to prohibit or restrain this execrable commerce."[59] Luther Martin

55 *Ibid.*, December 15, 1763; January 22, 1770.
56 *Ibid.*, January 4, 1768.
57 *New York Mercury*, November 14, 1774.
58 *Ibid.*
59 Hermann Von Holst, *Constitutional and Political History of the United States*, tr. J. Lalor, A. Mason, & P. Shorey (Chicago: Callaghan & Co., 1876-92), I, 282.

went one step further and denounced slaveholding itself as "inconsistent with the principles of the Revolution, and dishonorable to the American character."[60] Charles Thomson, the Secretary of the Continental Congress, scored the slave system as "a blot on our character that must be wiped out."[61] And John Jay, perhaps the staunchest advocate of antislavery in New York, declared that unless America was prepared to free the slaves "her own prayers to Heaven for liberty will be impious."[62]

Because slaveholders were generally responsive to antislavery appeals, manumissions increased sharply after 1774.[63] The bargaining power of the slaves also grew, for owners found it increasingly necessary to make concessions in order to obtain faithful service. In reporting this development, one newspaper observed that the slaves had become "infatuated with a desire of obtaining freedom."[64] Numerous agreements were recorded whereby slaves were given freedom in return for a stipulated term of loyal service.[65] And the privilege of approving prospective buyers was extended to include virtually all the slaves. This in turn enabled slaves to demand guarantees of eventual freedom before consenting to work for a new master.[66] Since such guarantees could be enforced against the buyer, they had the legal

[60] George, *Political History of Slavery*, pp. 9-10.
[61] *Rev. and Misc. Papers*, I, 214.
[62] Henry P. Johnston, ed., *The Correspondence and Public Papers of John Jay* (New York: G. P. Putnam's Sons, 1890-93), I, 406-7.
[63] Documents Book, XVIII, 115, MS. coll. East Hampton Free Library; Scrapbook, *passim*, MS. coll. East Hampton Free Library; Register of Manumissions, *passim;* Kingston Records, Manumissions, Hist. Docs. Coll., Klapper Library, Queens College; *Southold Town Records*, II, 445-46.
[64] *New York Mercury*, November 27, 1780.
[65] Register of Manumissions, pp. 63, 65, 66, *et seq.*
[66] *Ibid.*, pp. 43, 45, 171.

effect of raising many Negroes from the level of chattel bondage to the status of indentured servants.[67]

In the final analysis, military considerations were even more effective than ideology in undermining the slave system. The British occupation of southern New York thoroughly disrupted slave relations. Many supporters of the American cause were forced to abandon slaves and other property as they fled the British Army.[68] These slaves either merged with the free Negro population or left with the British at the end of the war. The British of course worked hard to drive a wedge between the Negro bondsmen and white supporters of the Revolution. In the bloody Tory-led raids in central New York slaves were not harmed unless they took arms to defend their masters.[69] By treating the slaves as neutrals, the British hoped to dampen Negro enthusiasm for the Revolution. In 1779 Sir Henry Clinton, the British Commander-in-Chief, made this standard policy by offering freedom to slaves who sought asylum with the British forces.[70]

The slaves who took up Clinton's offer were usually employed by the British in labor companies. Many were employed as wagon drivers and as laborers on the military works around New York City.[71] Indeed, so many were on the army payroll that the quartermaster made a fortune padding their wage receipts.[72] Some Negroes

[67] Wells v. Lane, 9 Johnson's Reports 144 (New York Supreme Court, 1812).

[68] Jacob E. Mallmann, ed., Historical Papers on Shelter Island and Its Presbyterian Church (New York: A. M. Bustard Co., 1899), p. 67.

[69] Jeptha R. Simms, The Frontiersmen of New York (Albany: George C. Riggs, 1882-83), II, 176.

[70] Royal Gazette, July 3, 1779.

[71] Proceedings of a Board of General Officers of the British Army at New York, 1781, in New-York Historical Society, Collections, XLIX (1916), 112, 118, 125-26, 130-31, 134, 136-37, 139, 141-42, 174, 210.

[72] Thomas Jones, History of New York during the Revolutionary War (New York: New-York Historical Society, 1879), I, 334.

were enlisted by the Tories in loyalist militia units in areas under British control.[73] So many ex-slaves were put under arms on Long Island in 1776 that Governor Trumbull of Connecticut feared that a foray was being organized against his state.[74] The cooperation of disaffected slaves was of great value to the British. Not only did runaways provide the British with valuable information, but they made a direct contribution to the British war effort.[75] In the Saratoga campaign hundreds of Negroes enlisted in the labor battalions attached to Burgoyne's army.[76] Although the British did not incorporate runaways into their regular combat formations, many Negroes saw action in the Loyal Refugees and other Tory military groups.[77]

British policy toward the slaves seriously handicapped the American war effort. From the beginning of hostilities New York authorities were deeply troubled about the subversion of the slave population.[78] An especially dangerous situation existed in northern New York, where British sympathizers encouraged desertion and sowed unrest generally. This sort of subversion pinned down militia badly needed in other places, for the authorities feared that the slaves would revolt if the troops left their home districts. The Albany Committee of Safety repeatedly refused to release its militia as long as unrest continued among the slaves.[79] The Committee clamped a tight curfew on Negroes and deported unruly slaves to New England, where the threat of subversion

[73] Peter Force, ed., *American Archives*, 5th Series (Washington: M. St. Clair Clarke & Peter Force, 1848-53), I, 486.
[74] *Ibid.*, II, 252.
[75] *Ibid.*, III, 1109.
[76] *Rev. and Misc. Papers*, III, 109.
[77] *New York Mercury*, February 11, 1782.
[78] *Journal of the New York Provincial Congress* (Albany: T. Weed, 1842), I, 215.
[79] Force, ed., *American Archives* (5th Series), III, 266.

was less immediate.[80] Similar measures were taken at Schenectady, where the Committee of Correspondence treated even minor offenses committed by the slaves as evidence of British subversion. Slaves venturing into the streets of Schenectady at night were severely flogged.[81] So much preoccupation with internal security inevitably impaired the military effectiveness of the Americans.

However deleterious its effect on military operations, the American preoccupation with security was fully justified by Tory efforts to undermine the loyalty of the slaves.[82] One Tory spy named Joseph Bettis was especially effective in spreading unrest. For several years Bettis's activities in and around Albany caused the authorities grave concern.[83] What they feared most was that the slaves might join the British prisoners being detained there in staging an uprising. As a precautionary measure the Albany council finally ordered all the prisoners of war to be moved out of the town.[84] These fears were generally well founded, for the slaves were only too willing to help the British. One bondsman was arrested in Albany in 1779 for "seducing a number of Negroes to join the enemy."[85] Another was ordered out of the county for attempting "to stir up the minds of the Negroes against their masters and raise insurrection among them."[86]

Numerous desertions combined with the ever-pres-

[80] *Minutes of the Albany Committee of Correspondence, 1775-1778* (Albany: University of the State of New York, 1923, 1925), I, 585, 954.

[81] *Minutes of the Schenectady Committee of Correspondence* (Albany: University of the State of New York, 1925), II, 1090.

[82] V. H. Paltsits, ed., *Minutes of the Commissioners for Detecting and Defeating Conspiracies in the State of New York* (Albany: Pub. by the State of New York [James B. Lyon Co., State printers], 1909-10), I, 142-43; II, 454-55, 702-3, 705-6. Hereinafter cited as *Min. of Comm. for Detecting Conspiracies.*

[83] *Ibid.*, II, 699-700, 741, 750, 762.

[84] Munsell, ed., *Collections on the History of Albany*, I, 282.

[85] *Min. of Comm. for Detecting Conspiracies*, I, 304.

[86] *Ibid.*

ent danger of insurrection forced the Americans to make important concessions to the slaves. Before the war was a year old, Americans had begun to emancipate bondsmen as a reward for military service. Washington, who had originally opposed the enlistment of Negroes, soon realized that only a policy of enlistment and emancipation could stem the tide of slaves flowing to the British.[87] By the end of hostilities more than four thousand Negroes had served in the Continental Army and thousands more in the local militia.[88] New York made a special effort to stimulate such enlistments. Slaves serving in any of the armed forces were given their freedom by statute after three years of service. The slaveowners were to be compensated with five hundred acres of public land for each slave who was allowed to enlist.[89] By giving the bondsman a personal stake in the war, the Americans won the support of thousands of Negroes who otherwise had no reason to support the American cause.

Negroes who took up the offer of freedom made an important contribution to the success of the Revolution in New York. One Hessian officer serving with Burgoyne observed of the American forces that "no regiment is to be seen in which there are not Negroes in abundance: And among them are able-bodied, strong, and brave fellows."[90] Even young Negro boys were enlisted as drummers in most of the New York regiments.[91] These Negroes gave a good account of them-

87 Force, ed., *American Archives* (4th Series), IV, 485.
88 W. E. Hartgrove, "The Negro Soldier in the American Revolution," *Journal of Negro History*, I (1916), 113-19.
89 *Laws of New York, 1781*, XXXII.
90 August Schlozer, *Briefwechsel* (Göttingen: Vandenhoek, 1780-82), IV, 365.
91 *Journal of Lieutenant Charles Philip Von Krafft, of the Regiment of Van Bose, 1776-1784*, in New-York Historical Society, *Collections*, XL (1882), 183.

selves wherever they fought. In 1781 Colonel Christopher Greene's Negro regiment distinguished itself at Points Bridge in one of the sharpest and bloodiest local actions of the war.[92] The British conceded the effectiveness of American Negro troops in 1779 when they warned that Negroes captured in military actions would henceforth be sold into slavery regardless of their legal status.[93] The British in effect offered freedom to slaves who joined them and threatened free men who opposed them with slavery. Like the Americans, their attitude toward slavery was guided mainly by expediency rather than by ideology.

Both the Americans and the British made good on their promises to the slaves who joined them. In 1781 the New York Assembly passed a law freeing all Negroes serving in the state's armed forces.[94] The British likewise kept faith. General Sir Guy Carleton, who negotiated the British evacuation of New York City at the end of the war, adopted the following policy: Negroes with the British prior to the signing of the provisional peace treaty on November 30, 1782, were free; those seeking refuge after that date were to be given up.[95] Despite great pressure from the Americans that all fugitives be returned, Carleton refused to break the promises of freedom that had been made during the war. To do so, he said, would be "a dishonorable violation of the public faith."[96] Altogether three thousand Negroes offi-

[92] Samuel G. Arnold, *History of Rhode Island* (New York: D. Appleton & Co., 1874), II, 427-28.

[93] *New York Mercury*, July 5, 1779.

[94] *Laws of New York, 1781*, XXXII.

[95] Benjamin Quarles, *The Negro in the American Revolution* (Chapel Hill: Pub. for the Institute of Early American History and Culture, Williamsburg, Va., by the University of North Carolina Press, 1961), p. 171.

[96] *Ibid.*, pp. 168-69.

cially left with the British besides hundreds of others who left unrecorded in private vessels.[97]

The policies pursued by both sides during the Revolution inevitably undermined the whole slave system. The slaves took advantage of the white man's war to support one side or the other as it happened to serve their interests. Whether they deserted to the British or enlisted with the Americans, the bondsmen used the conflict to loosen their own shackels. That they should seize any opportunity that came along to win freedom was consistent with the whole history of slavery in New York. Slaves who over the years had worked and bargained to obtain emancipation jumped at the chance to play one side off against the other in order to achieve their objective. All that mattered to the slaves was that the Revolution offered a golden opportunity to escape from bondage. The way they seized the opportunity left no doubt as to how much they valued liberty.

[97] *Ibid.*, p. 172.

IX. ABOLITION

"WITHIN 20 YEARS THE OPINION OF THE IN-
JUSTICE OF SLAVE HOLDING HAS BECOME
ALMOST UNIVERSAL."
—*William Dunlap to Thomas Holcroft, July 29, 1797.*

SLAVERY came under direct political attack
in 1777 when the opponents of slavery obtained a
clear majority in New York's first Constitutional Convention. Although the idea of outright emancipation
was rejected as impolitic during wartime, the principle
of eventual emancipation was endorsed by the majority. The delegates adopted a policy statement proposed by Gouverneur Morris which committed New
York to the principle that "every human being who
breathes the air of the state shall enjoy the privileges of
a freeman." The resolution urged future legislatures "to
take the most effective measures consistent with public
safety for abolishing domestic slavery." So great was the
sentiment against continuing slavery as a permanent
institution that only five of the thirty-six delegates present failed to support the antislavery resolution.[1]

No legislative action was taken, however, until
1781, when the legislature voted to manumit slaves who
were serving in the armed forces.[2] Another four years
passed before any action was taken to implement the
Convention's resolution on eventual emancipation. The
long delay is mainly attributable to the unsettled condi-

[1] *Journal of the New York Provincial Congress*, I, 887-89.
[2] *Laws of New York, 1781*, XXXII.

tions which resulted from military operations in New York. To enact drastic social changes while the war was on might conceivably play into the hands of the enemy. The legislature therefore, with an eye to the "public safety" proviso in the antislavery resolution, hesitated to act on any proposal for general emancipation until normal conditions were restored in the state.

By 1785, when the legislature was at last ready to take up the problem of emancipation, there was a clear antislavery majority in both houses. Considerable disagreement existed, however, over the means to be adopted for implementing emancipation. A bill for gradual emancipation was offered in the Assembly which provided that children born to slave women after 1785 should be free from birth. Before this bill could be brought to a vote, a militant group of antislavery representatives led by Aaron Burr proposed the immediate and unconditional abolition of slavery. The Assembly rejected Burr's proposal 33–13, and approved the more moderate plan for gradual emancipation by a vote of 36–11.[3] The latter vote, though certainly decisive, does not reflect the full voting strength of antislavery in the lower house. Ten of the representatives opposed to the moderate plan had previously voted for Burr's far more radical proposal. Thus the Assembly actually voted 46–1 in favor of some form of emancipation.[4] Almost unanimous on the desirability of emancipation, the representatives only disagreed as to how it might best be effected.[5]

That the legislature in the end failed to provide for emancipation in 1785 can be traced to the refusal of the

3 *Journal of the Assembly of the State of New York*, February 25, 1785.
4 *Ibid.*
5 *Ibid.*, March 1, 1785.

162

Assembly to separate the emancipation question from
the broader issue of civil rights for Negroes. Many of the
representatives were frankly worried about the political and social ramifications of emancipation. Although
in favor of emancipation, they hesitated to give Negroes
full civil equality with the white population. The bill
which finally emerged from the Assembly contained a
number of riders invidious to the rights of free Negroes.
Negroes were denied the right to vote or hold public
office, forbidden to intermarry with white persons, and
barred from giving testimony against whites in any
court of the state.[6] The representatives in effect sought
to blunt the political and social impact of emancipation
by relegating the Negro freedmen to a civil limbo of
second-class citizenship.

This attempt to hedge emancipation with racial restrictions found almost no support in the Senate. A
majority of the upper house rejected the discriminatory
riders attached to the Assembly's bill. The Senate went
on record against any emancipation plan which discrim-
inated against free Negroes on the basis of race. The
senators were convinced that racial restrictions were not
only unfair to the Negro but generally unsound from
the standpoint of public policy. Such restrictions would
only perpetuate distrust between the races and ultimately result in civil disorder. The Senate therefore
deleted the discriminatory riders and sent the bill back
to the Assembly for reconsideration.[7]

The Senate's strong stand in favor of civil equality
induced the Assembly to abandon its restrictions on
intermarriage, the right of free Negroes to hold public
office, and the admissibility of Negro testimony in the

6 *Ibid.*, March 9, 1785.
7 *Ibid.*, March 9, 12, 1785.

courts.[8] But the Assembly refused to give way on the issue of Negro suffrage. A revised bill approved by the Assembly as a committee of the whole was passed with a rider which retained the original ban on Negro voting.[9] By its action the Assembly served notice that there would be no emancipation law which did not include a voting restriction. In order to break the impending deadlock which threatened to block emancipation, the Senate reluctantly accepted the Assembly's terms and agreed to the suffrage proviso.[10]

With both houses finally in agreement, the emancipation bill would have become law but for the strong opposition of the Council of Revision to its discriminatory provisions. Chancellor Livingston was a leading spokesman against the bill in the Council. Negroes could not, he said, "be deprived of these essential rights without shocking the principle of equal liberty which every page in that Constitution labors to enforce."[11] The Council in the end rejected the bill, returning it to the legislature with an advisory message excoriating the proposed franchise restriction.[12] The Council warned that restrictions which drew a legal distinction between classes of citizens on the basis of race were divisive and dangerous. It warned that the proposed suffrage restriction would undermine the civic morale of Negroes generally by depriving them of an effective political voice. The Council feared that a political quarantine might turn Negroes into a subversive force, aliens from the rest

8 Ibid.
9 Ibid., March 12, 1785.
10 Journal of the Senate of the State of New York, March 12, 1785.
11 Quoted in Alfred B. Street, The Council of Revision of the State of New York (Albany: W. Gould, 1859), p. 268. For Livingston's advocacy of antislavery and Negro rights, see George Dangerfield, Chancellor Robert R. Livingston of New York, 1746-1813 (New York: Harcourt, Brace, 1960), p. 451.
12 Journal of the Senate, March 12, 1785.

of society, without a stake in the processes of orderly government. It urged the legislature to do nothing that would interfere with the assimilation of free Negroes into the political and social life of the community. The Council warned that racial discrimination was as dangerous to the long-run interests of the white population as it was unjust to the Negro.[13]

The Council's message had no apparent effect on the Senate.[14] Although most of the senators agreed in principle with the Council, the majority wanted immediate action on emancipation even if it required acceptance of an undesirable suffrage restriction. Disregarding the Council's advice, the Senate passed the bill and sent it on to the Assembly confident that similar action would be taken there.[15] The Assembly, however, was no longer sure just what it wanted. A majority of the representatives now agreed with the Council that racial disfranchisement was dangerous and undesirable, yet they could not bring themselves to vote for emancipation without it. Unable to break the dilemma of their own making, they voted to sustain the Council's veto and defer action on emancipation. Thus the bill lost by a vote of 23–17 because of the very suffrage restriction that the majority had insisted upon.[16] In the final analysis, emancipation was blocked by a majority which feared Negro suffrage more than it desired emancipation.

This unexpected setback was a bitter disappointment to opponents of slavery, who now intensified their demands for antislavery legislation. Their pressure led

13 *Journal of the Assembly*, March 26, 1785.

14 Bills disapproved by the Council of Revision were returned to the legislature, which could enact them into law by a simple majority. Since the bill went to the Council from the Senate, it was returned to that body for reconsideration before going to the Assembly, where it had in fact originated.

15 *Journal of the Senate*, March 21, 1785.

16 *Journal of the Assembly*, March 26, 1785.

the legislature to enact several statutes against the slave trade. Thus a law was passed in 1785 which prohibited the importation of slaves under penalty of a fine of £100 for the importer and freedom for the slave.[17] The law, however, applied only to slaves imported for sale, so persons bringing in slaves for their own use were not affected. Three years later in 1788 the legislature completely outlawed the slave trade with a law which provided that "slaves exported or attempted to be exported shall be free."[18] The Act of 1785 against the importation of slaves was also strengthened to provide that if a master sold a slave who had been brought into the state for his own use, the sale would operate to free the slave.[19]

Further evidence of the growing strength of antislavery can be found in a sweeping revision of the slave controls, enacted by the legislature in 1788. The revised code permitted owners to manumit slaves without posting a bond if the slave was under fifty years of age and not likely to become a public charge. It was left up to the local overseers of the poor to determine whether a slave being proposed for manumission qualified under the new regulations. The manumission bond was also waived for testamentary emancipations if the overseers were satisfied that the slave was in good health and capable of self-support. Negroes who subsequently became a public charge were to remain free and any expense incurred by the county for their support was to be charged against the testator's estate.[20]

The revised code liberalized the slave controls and extended to slaves legal privileges previously reserved

17 *Laws of New York, 1785,* LXVIII.
18 *Ibid., 1788,* XL.
19 *Ibid.*
20 *Ibid.*

to the whites. The law now gave the right of jury trial to slaves in all cases involving the death penalty.[21] This ended forever the special slave courts of three justices and five freeholders which for eighty years had primary jurisdiction over slaves charged with capital crimes.[22] The terroristic punishments of the colonial era were also abolished and slaves charged with capital offenses were brought within the regular penalties prescribed by law for white offenders.[23] The net effect of the revised code was to end the double standard of justice in New York and to extend to the Negro slaves the same laws and judicial procedures that covered the white population.

The action taken by the legislature against slavery encouraged the relaxation of the local slave controls. Whatever brutality may have existed before virtually disappeared in everyday slave relations. Corporal punishment was rarely inflicted on slaves who violated municipal slave ordinances. At Albany the town council abolished flogging for infractions of the curfew, by far the most important of the slave controls. Instead of flogging the offending slave, the council ordered a fine levied against his owner.[24] Private discipline also relaxed. Public opinion generally restrained owners from punishing their slaves severely regardless of the provocation. Some owners indeed preferred to manumit especially troublesome slaves rather than to resort to forms of discipline condemned by the community.[25]

These attacks on slavery found strong support in the general community. In the 1780's opponents of slavery

21 *Ibid.*
22 *Supra*, p. 92.
23 *Laws of New York, 1788*, XL.
24 Munsell, ed., *Collections on the History of Albany*, II, 379-81.
25 Edward A. Collier, *A History of Old Kinderhook* (New York: G. P. Putnam's Sons, 1914), p. 210.

intensified their efforts throughout the state. The New York press, always a good barometer of public opinion in the late eighteenth century, took an increasingly militant antislavery line.[26] The *New York Gazetteer* attacked slavery as "the deprivation of all the rights which nature has given to man."[27] It singled out the slave trade for special attack as "cruel, wicked, and diabolical."[28] The *New York Journal* informed its readers that slaveowners deserved to be plundered, tormented, and even massacred by the avenging hands of their purchased slaves."[29] Other papers followed an antislavery line in general by publishing tracts and articles impugning the morality of slaveholding.[30] These newspapers played a vital role in crystallizing antislavery sentiment. Their editorial broadsides kept the issue before the public and increased the pressure on state officials for emancipation.

But the most effective single agency of antislavery in the state was the New York Manumission Society. Organized in 1785 to rally support for the emancipation bill, the Society was sponsored by some of the most distinguished citizens of the state. John Jay was the first president and Alexander Hamilton the second. Its founding members included Melancton Smith, St. John de Crèvecœur, Philip Schuyler, James Duane, and Chancellor Livingston.[31] Although the Society failed to obtain an emancipation law in 1785, it was important that prominent men spoke out on the issue and made their own position clear. The failure of the legislature

26 *New York Journal and State Gazette,* April 15, 1784; *New York Journal, or the Weekly Register,* January 26, August 10, 1786.
27 *New York Gazetteer,* February 4, 1785.
28 *Ibid.,* February 15, 1785.
29 *New York Journal, or the Weekly Register,* June 22, 1786.
30 *Poughkeepsie Journal,* December 22, 1789.
31 Minutes of the New York Manumission Society, February 4, 1785, MS. coll. N.Y. Hist. Soc.

to pass the emancipation bill demonstrated that much organized effort, including heavy pressure on state officials, would be needed to win the fight against slavery. The Society was the real working organization of the antislavery movement. It kept the issue before the public by circulating petitions, awarding prizes for antislavery tracts, sponsoring lectures and orations, printing and distributing large quantities of antislavery literature, and exposing violations of the laws against the slave trade.[32] The latter absorbed much of its time, for slaves continued to be brought into the state for sale under various subterfuges. Some owners evaded the law by leasing imported slaves instead of selling them outright. These "leases" were actually disguised sales which could be cancelled only with the consent of the hirer or his heirs.[33] Others evaded the law by manumitting their slaves while retaining the right to their services under long indentures. One importer brought in a "free" Negro from New Jersey under a ninety-nine year indenture.[34] And since the law did not prohibit sales by legal representatives of the owner, imported slaves could still be sold by executors or administrators, by assignees of absent or insolvent debtors, by sheriffs at forced sales, and by trustees.[35] These exceptions provided so many opportunities for fraud that the utmost vigilance was needed to enforce the law.

[32] *Ibid.*, February 15, 1787; September 24, 1788; August 20, 1789; May 15, 1792; *New York Gazetteer*, February 18, 1785; January 15, 1787; *New York Journal, or the Weekly Register*, October 26, November 9, 1786.

[33] *Sable v. Hitchcock*, 2 Johnson's Cases 79 (New York Supreme Court, 1800).

[34] Minutes of the New York Manumission Society, June 23, 1795.

[35] *Sable v. Hitchcock*, 2 Johnson's Cases 79 (New York Supreme Court, 1800); *Caesar v. Peabody*, 11 Johnson's Cases 68 (New York Supreme Court, 1814).

Another violation which the Society worked hard to prevent was the illegal export of slaves from the state. The demand for labor in the South was so great that traders scoured New York for slaves. After all commissions, insurance costs, and shipping charges had been paid, an able-bodied slave could be sold in the southern market for a profit of at least £40.[36] The traffic attained such proportions in the 1780's that the Society took special preventive measures. Watchers were appointed for different parts of the state to report any unusual purchases of slaves by outsiders. The Society also kept ships known to participate in the slave trade under close surveillance while they were in port.[37]

But the most important work of the Society from both a practical and polemical standpoint was the assistance given to free Negroes illegally held in bondage. Unscrupulous whites took advantage of every opportunity to victimize Negroes, and as long as slavery existed as a domestic institution such opportunities were numerous. Young Negroes apprenticed to white artisans were sometimes sold as chattels in plain violation of the law. Others were enticed into debt by sharpers who charged usurious rates and then sold their victims into slavery when they were unable to pay.[38] No one can ever estimate how many Negroes were deprived of their freedom by one ruse or another, but in just one year the Society processed thirty-three cases of unlawful enslavement.[39] The Society provided such Negroes with legal counsel, helped them to regain their freedom, and

36 Minutes of the New York Manumission Society, November 10, 1785; Thomas Morris's Certificate of Sale, September 27, 1784, MS. coll. N.Y. Hist. Soc.
37 Minutes of the New York Manumission Society, June 22, 1792; January 11, 1793.
38 *Ibid.*, February 11, June 20, August 28, 1794; April 20, May 25, 1797.
39 *Ibid.*, March 21, 1797.

in some cases recovered damages to compensate them for their unlawful detention.[40]

The Society was able to mount powerful economic pressure against slavery by organizing boycotts against those who participated in the slave trade. Warnings were given to merchants, vendue masters, and newspaper owners that those who involved themselves in the trade could expect economic reprisals.[41] The antislavery line taken by the newspapers can be traced in part to this sort of economic intimidation. The Society had a special committee of antislavery militants who visited newspaper offices from time to time to remind publishers of the unwisdom of accepting advertisements for the purchase or sale of slaves.[42] Another committee kept a list of persons who either participated or invested in the slave trade.[43] The list was carefully kept up to date and opponents of slavery were urged to boycott anyone listed. Such tactics were very convincing arguments to the business class that even tacit support given to slavery could be costly.

The effectiveness of the Society was reflected in the rapid progress of antislavery everywhere in the state. The press responded to the campaign with articles and editorials attacking involuntary servitude as "contrary to the idea of liberty this country has so happily established."[44] It is significant that after 1790 slave auctions practically disappeared and that the few which were held usually attracted more critics than buyers. A public sale of several slaves at Whitestone in 1796 was attacked by a Long Island newspaper as "disgraceful to humanity." Readers of the paper were urged to protest against

40 *Ibid.*, April 16, 1795; March 11, 1800.
41 *Ibid.*, November 20, 1788; August 18, 1795.
42 *Ibid.*, August 18, 1790.
43 *Ibid.*, May 18, 1790.
44 *The Independent Journal*, January 24, 1784.

the "outrage" by sending petitions to the legislature.[45] Everywhere the tide ran strongly against slavery. Writing in 1797, the New York diarist Dunlap observed that "within 20 years the opinion of the injustice of slave holding has become almost universal."[46] Economic and social changes at work in the state complemented ideology in promoting antislavery. The second half of the eighteenth century in New York was marked by a high birth rate, as well as by a sharp rise in white immigration from other colonies.[47] As a result, the supply of free labor increased much more rapidly in this period than the slave force. By 1771 the ratio of Negro slaves to whites in the total population had declined to its lowest point in 68 years.[48] During the next fifteen years the free population increased about 47 per cent while the slave population decreased about 5 per cent. In 1771 the ratio of slaves to whites was about one to seven, whereas in 1786 the ratio had declined to one to twelve.[49]

The rapid increase of the free population made slavery a relatively uneconomic system of labor. The

[45] *Frothingham's Long Island Herald,* January 11, 1796.
[46] *Dunlap's Diary,* I, 119.
[47] E. Wilder Spaulding, *New York in the Critical Period* (New York: Columbia University Press, 1932), pp. 30-31.

[48]

Year	Per Cent Slave	Year	Per Cent Slave
1703	11.5	1746	14.8
1723	14.8	1749	14.4
1731	14.3	1756	14.0
1737	14.7	1771	11.8

Statistics compiled from Greene and Harrington, *American Population before 1790,* pp. 95-102.

[49]

Year	Whites	Slaves	Per Cent Slave
1771	148,124	19,883	11.8
1786	219,996	18,889	7.9

Statistics compiled from *ibid.,* pp. 102-3.

172

costs of slavery were high both from the standpoint of the master's initial investment and the continuous expense of maintaining slaves during periods of idleness. Free labor, on the other hand, could be hired and discharged at will, for the employer had no financial stake in the plight of his workers during periods of unemployment. As the supply of free labor increased and the wage rate fell, slavery became an obsolete and expensive system of labor. The rapid progress of antislavery after the Revolution partly reflected the changing character of the New York labor force. The ideal of freedom was an important motive force, but the increased availability of cheap free labor was an important factor in its widespread acceptance.

The increased importance of free labor was reflected in a sharp rise in manumissions and the entry of numerous Negroes into the labor market.[50] From the beginning the Manumission Society assisted these freedmen in the often difficult task of adjusting to life in the free community. Schools were established to teach Negro children reading, writing, arithmetic, and geography, as well as vocational subjects. The Society also maintained a free evening school where adults were given vocational instruction.[51] Such schools eased the transition from slavery to freedom by preparing Negroes for the employment opportunities created by the increased demand for wage labor. The heavy volume of newspaper advertisements for Negro workers indicates that such opportunities were numerous.[52] The Society

[50] Documents Book, XVIII, 115, MS. coll. East Hampton Free Library; Kingston Records, Manumissions, 1794-1811, Hist. Docs. Coll., Klapper Library, Queens College; Register of Manumissions, *passim; Southold Town Records,* II, 445-46, 449-50.

[51] Minutes of the New York Manumission Society, August 8, November 15, 20, 1787; January 17, 1797.

[52] *The Independent Journal,* May 19, 1784; *New York Journal & Patriotic Register,* April 6, December 21, 1799; *The Royal Gazette,*

estimated that in 1797 over two thousand free Negroes were employed in a wide variety of occupations in New York City alone.[53]

Several religious denominations, especially the Quakers and Presbyterians, supported the efforts of the Manumission Society to facilitate the transition from slavery to freedom. In the 1780's the Quakers of Flushing set up a committee to help freedmen who required assistance.[54] The Quaker congregation at Chappaqua voted to compensate Negroes formerly held as slaves by Quakers for the service they had rendered in bondage.[55] The Presbyterians, though not as militant as the Quakers in opposing slavery, nevertheless worked hard to prepare for the transition to freedom. The state synod urged Presbyterians to give their slaves "such good education as to prepare them for a better employment of freedom."[56] By constantly reminding New Yorkers of the slavery issue, such appeals helped to create pro-emancipation sentiment throughout the state.

The legal extinction of slavery finally began in 1799 when the legislature passed a statute abolishing slavery through a system of gradual manumission. The law freed all children born to slave women after July 4, 1799, the males to become free at the age of twenty-

---

July 13, August 21, 1782; *New York Morning Post*, October 15, 1787; *New York Mercury*, January 13, 1772; June 29, August 17, 1778; October 11, 1779; May 27, 1782; June 30, 1783; *et seq.*

53 *Minutes of the Proceedings of the Fourth Convention of Delegates from the Abolition Societies Established in Different Parts of the United States Assembled at Philadelphia on the Third Day of May, One Thousand Seven Hundred and Ninety-seven, and Continued, by Appointments, until the Ninth Day of the Same Month, Inclusive* (Philadelphia, 1797), pp. 29-31. Cited in Dwight Dumond, *Antislavery: The Crusade for Freedom in America* (Ann Arbor: University of Michigan Press, 1961), p. 42.

54 Baird, *History of Rye*, p. 188.

55 Sharf, *History of Westchester County*, I, 30.

56 Quoted in Woodson, *The Education of the Negro prior to 1861*, p. 74.

eight, and females at the age of twenty-five. Slaveholders were required to register all children born to their slave women after this date under penalty of a fine for the owner and immediate freedom for the child. Children who were properly registered were to be the indentured servants of the slaveowner until they reached the statutory age. The owner, however, could waive his claim to them at any time, as well as his responsibility for their support, by assigning them to the local overseers of the poor.[57] No attempt was made by any of the lawmakers to hedge emancipation with political or social restrictions. The question of the Negro's civil status was kept separate from the question of emancipation. By avoiding all discussion of the racial issues which had deadlocked the legislature fourteen years before, the sponsors of the statute were able to guide it through both houses with only token opposition.[58]

Gradual emancipation in turn gave rise to numerous problems of enforcement. The demand for labor in the slave states was such that a lucrative business sprang

[57] *Laws of New York, 1799*, LXII; *ibid., 1801*, CLXXXVIII.

[58] The Gradual Manumission Act has been described by Dixon Ryan Fox as a Federalist measure passed by a straight party vote of 68-23 in the Assembly. The vote cited by Fox, however, was not on the bill as a whole but only on a particular clause which manumitted slave children born after July 4, 1799, and which provided that they should be held as bond servants for a statutory period. Because this clause contained in fact two separate provisions—one enacting emancipation and the other providing for indentured servitude—there is no way to determine whether the members voting in the negative were opposed to one or the other provision or both. But that the vote did not follow straight party lines is certain, for Aaron Burr voted with the majority. As the leader of the Tammany Society, Burr was not in the habit of voting with Federalists on party measures. Moreover, since the complete bill was enacted by both houses *viva voce*, there is no possible way to determine from the vote whether it was more strongly supported by the Federalists or by the Republicans. See *Journal of the Senate*, March 25, 27, 1799, and *Journal of the Assembly*, March 28, 1799. Cf. Fox, "The Negro Vote in Old New York," *Political Science Quarterly*, XXXII (1917), 254.

175

up in the export of Negroes to the South. Because the Gradual Manumission Act depressed slave values within the state, traders were able to purchase slaves at bargain prices for illegal sale elsewhere. Moreover, there were many slaveowners who exploited every technicality in the law in order to squeeze a final profit out of slavery. The law could be evaded, for instance, by sending pregnant slave women out of the state until they had given birth and returning them to New York after the infants had been sold. In this way unscrupulous owners were able to circumvent the law without the slightest risk of being prosecuted.[59]

How many Negroes were sent out of the state illegally cannot be estimated with precision, for the traffic was necessarily surreptitious. Nevertheless, there is strong indirect evidence which points to the conclusion that the number was large. The federal census reveals an extremely sharp drop in the growth rate of New York's Negro population after 1800. During the period from 1810 to 1830 the rate of increase fell to .57 per cent yearly as compared with 2.13 per cent for the decade prior to 1800. Negroes in 1790 accounted for 7.6 per cent of the total population; by 1830 this percentage had fallen to 2.3.[60] Since there is no evidence that the birth rate fell off precipitously after 1800, it seems obvious that Negroes left the state in considerable numbers. Moreover, since the civil status of free Negroes was better in New York than in most places, it is unlikely that many left voluntarily. The conclu-

59 *Laws of New York, 1785,* LXVIII. These evasions were also common in other northern states which had provided for gradual emancipation. See Edward R. Turner, *The Negro in Pennsylvania: Slavery, Servitude, Freedom, 1639-1861* (Washington: The American Historical Association, 1911), p. 80.

60 United States Census Bureau, *Negroes in the United States, 1790-1915* (Washington: Government Printing Office, 1935), pp. 11, 15-16.

sion is inescapable that the exodus was largely the work of kidnappers and illegal traders who dealt in human misery.

Both state and local officials tried with mixed success to stamp out this miserable traffic. A law passed in 1801 provided that no one could leave the state with slaves purchased less than one year previously, and after 1807 the period was extended to ten years.[61] In 1805 New York City denied the use of its jails for the detention of alleged fugitives.[62] And the courts gave an increasingly antislavery construction to the laws against the slave trade. They construed these laws to include runaways in order to free fugitives from other states who had been recovered and later sold in New York. They struck down long-standing methods of evasion by freeing slaves brought into the state for hire, as well as Negroes "manumitted" in other states and brought to New York under long indentures as servants.[63] They even reversed their own rule regarding executory emancipation agreements and freed slaves who had been promised freedom even where no formal act of manumission had taken place.[64]

The illicit traffic in Negroes caused enough public indignation to speed up the extinction of slavery. The kidnappers and sharpers who traded in human misery demonstrated that as long as the status of any Negro remained in doubt no Negro would be safe. The result

[61] *Public Laws of the State of New York Passed at the Second Meeting of the Twenty-Fourth Session of the Legislature, 1801* (Albany: 1801), pp. 548-49. Cited in Dumond, *Antislavery*, p. 50.

[62] *Minutes of the Common Council, 1784-1831* (New York: M. B. Brown, 1917), III, 691.

[63] *Fish v. Fisher*, 2 Johnson's Cases 89 (New York Supreme Court, 1800); *In re Tom*, 5 Johnson's Reports 365 (New York Supreme Court, 1810); *Sable v. Hitchcock*, 2 Johnson's Cases 79 (New York Supreme Court, 1800).

[64] *Wells v. Lane*, 9 Johnson's Reports 144 (New York Supreme Court, 1812).

was a stream of legislation resolving the issue in favor of freedom. In 1809 the state recognized slave marriages, legitimized the children of slaves, and prohibited the separation of spouses.[65] Another law passed in 1809 recognized the right of slaves to own and transfer property by will.[66] Four years later the colonial legislation barring Negroes from giving testimony against whites was repealed and slaves accused of crimes were given the right to a jury trial.[67] Finally, in 1817 every slave born before July 4, 1799 was freed as of July 4, 1827.[68] Since the emancipation of slaves born after 1799 had already been provided for, the Act of 1817 set the stage for the complete extinction of slavery.

This did not occur until fourteen years later, however, for the law contained an exception which permitted nonresidents to enter New York with their slaves for periods up to nine months.[69] Thus slaves could be brought into the state long after slavery had been outlawed as a local institution. But the significance of this exception was in fact negligible, for the antislavery attitude of the New York courts discouraged slaveowners from exercising it. In 1834 the highest court of the state declared that local laws authorizing the detention of runaways were unconstitutional because Congress had already pre-empted this area of legislation under the federal fugitive slave law.[70] The upshot of

65 *Public Laws of the State of New York Passed at the Thirty-Second Session of the Legislature* (Albany, 1809), p. 450. Cited in Dumond, *Antislavery*, p. 50.

66 *Laws of New York, 1809,* LVIV.

67 William P. Van Ness and John Woodworth, eds., *Laws of the State of New York, Revised and Passed at the Thirty-Sixth Session of the Legislature* (Albany: H. C. Southwick & Co., 1813), II, 207.

68 *Laws of New York, 1817,* CXXXVII.

69 *Ibid.*

70 *Jack v. Martin,* 12 Wendell's Reports 311 (New York Court for the Correction of Errors, 1834).

this decision was that few owners would risk bringing slaves into New York under any circumstances. The privilege nevertheless technically remained in effect for another seven years until the emergence of slavery as a national issue made its continuance repugnant to most New Yorkers. Its repeal in 1841 erased the last vestiges of slavery from the life of the state.[71]

[71] *Laws of New York, 1841*, CCXLVII.

X. THE FAILURE
OF FREEDOM

"I RECOLLECT THAT WHILE PURSUING MY JOUR-
NEY, I OVERTOOK A WHITE MAN DRIVING A
SPAN OF HORSES, WHO CONTENDED THAT I
HAD NOT A RIGHT TO TRAVEL THE PUBLIC
HIGHWAY AS OTHER MEN DID, BUT THAT IT
WAS MY PLACE TO KEEP BEHIND HIM AND HIS
TEAM."

—*Austin Steward*[1]

Ⅰ N the late eighteenth century the antislavery
movement generally followed a similar pattern throughout the North. The first restrictions imposed on slavery regulated and eventually abolished the foreign and
domestic slave trade.[2] A further step toward abolition
came with the formation of antislavery societies through
which northern opponents of slavery rallied public
support for the movement. And, as in New York, the
newspapers played a crucial role in promoting the
movement by maintaining pressure on state officials for
emancipation.[3] Everywhere in the North slavery came
under attack as alien to the ideals of the Revolution
and inimical to the future of the country.[4] In rapid

---

[1] Austin Steward, *Twenty-Two Years a Slave and Forty Years a Freeman* (Rochester: William Alling, 1857), 124-25.

[2] *Session Laws of New Jersey, 1786*, p. 239; *Laws of Pennsylvania,
1788*, CXLIX; *Acts and Laws of Connecticut, 1788*, p. 368; *Acts and
Resolves of Rhode Island, October, 1799*, p. 6.

[3] William D. Johnston, *Slavery in Rhode Island, 1755-1776* (Providence: Rhode Island Historical Society, 1894), pp. 36-39.

[4] Henry S. Cooley, *A Study of Slavery in New Jersey* (Baltimore:

succession six states—Connecticut, Massachusetts, New Hampshire, Vermont, Rhode Island, and Pennsylvania —abolished slavery before the ratification of the federal Constitution.[5] New York began statutory emancipation in 1799, and New Jersey—the last northern state to legislate against slavery—adopted a program of gradual emancipation in 1804.[6]

Whites in the North overwhelmingly supported the antislavery movement, though not always for the same reasons. Upper-class whites were motivated by idealism, and their attitude toward the Negro was philanthropic and paternalistic. Members of the upper class supported Negro charities and schools much more generously than they supported organizations assisting poor whites. The proliferation of Negro philanthropies everywhere in the North reflected the near obsession of the wealthy with the slavery issue. John Jay, one of the leaders of the New York aristocracy, purchased slaves and, after training them to earn a livelihood, gave them their freedom.[7] Antislavery became in effect a class crusade for the domestic application of the natural rights doctrine to the Negro. The propertied class in general regarded the emancipation movement as a logical sequel to their own recent struggle for political freedom. The intensity of their commitment made the New York Manumission Society and similar organizations through-

Johns Hopkins University Press, 1896), pp. 21-23; Turner, *The Negro in Pennsylvania*, pp. 77-78; Johnston, *Slavery in Rhode Island*, pp. 36-39.

5 *Laws of Pennsylvania, 1780*, CXLVI; *Acts and Laws of Connecticut, 1784*, pp. 233-34; *Acts and Resolves of Rhode Island, February 1784*, pp. 6-8; *Massachusetts Constitution of 1780*, Article I; *Vermont Constitution of 1777*, Article I; *New Hampshire Constitution of 1783*, Article I.

6 *Session Laws of New Jersey, 1804*, p. 251.

7 George Pellew, *John Jay* (New York: Houghton, Mifflin & Co., 1898), pp. 293-94.

out the North highly effective instruments of anti-slavery.[8]

This idealism had no counterpart in the lower classes, among whom could be found neither sympathy for the Negro nor understanding of his problems. From its inception, slavery had been detrimental to the working class. On the one hand, the slave system excluded whites from jobs pre-empted by slaves; on the other, it often degraded them socially to the level of the slaves with whom they had to work and compete in earning a livelihood. Many whites preferred chauvinistic idleness to employment which had come to be identified with slavery.[9] The working class recognized slavery for what it was—a system that had long impoverished and degraded them.[10] But their response as a class was irrational, for in reacting against slavery they succumbed to an unreasoning antipathy for the Negro as the embodiment of the system. Whites in effect blamed the Negro for a system of exploitation which made Negroes its principal victims.

Whites of the working class hated slavery as an institution, but they also feared the free Negro as an economic competitor. They supported emancipation not to raise the Negro to a better life but to destroy a system which gave him a fixed place in the economy. As John Adams observed of the white working class in Massachusetts, "they would not suffer the labour by which alone they could obtain subsistence to be done by slaves."[11] The self-serving character of workingclass attitudes to-

[8] Minutes of the New York Manumission Society, February 4, 1785; May 17, November 17, 1787; May 15, 1792; February 11, August 28, 1794; et seq.

[9] Nathaniel Appleton, Considerations on Slavery, in Slavery Pamphlets, E411, Box A12, N.Y. Hist. Soc.

[10] Steward, Twenty-Two Years a Slave, pp. 125, 167.

[11] John Adams to Jeremy Belknap (1795), Belknap Papers, in Massachusetts Historical Society, Collections, 5th Ser., III, 402.

ward emancipation can be seen in much of the antislavery legislation of the late eighteenth century. New Jersey prohibited the importation of slaves in 1786 because "sound public policy requires that importation be prohibited in order that white labour may be protected."[12] In prohibiting the importation of slaves, the Connecticut legislature declared that "the increase of slaves is injurious to the poor."[13] Often the rationale of antislavery had nothing to do with the welfare of the Negro —indeed, as in the case of Connecticut and New Jersey, it was unabashedly hostile to the Negro.

Northern antipathy for the Negro was reflected in a number of racial restrictions enacted by the states. Connecticut prohibited free schools for nonresident Negroes on the ground that such schools "would tend to the great increase of the colored people of the state and thereby to the injury of the people."[14] Massachusetts, Rhode Island, and Maine prohibited marriage between Negroes and whites.[15] Massachusetts prohibited nonresident Negroes to remain in the state for longer than two months under penalty of flogging.[16] In Pennsylvania the courts ruled that Negroes were not citizens and therefore not eligible to vote.[17] Both New Jersey and Connecticut amended their constitutions in order to disfranchise free Negroes.[18] Rhode Island denied Negroes the right to become freemen of the towns, thereby

12 *Session Laws of New Jersey, 1786,* p. 239.
13 *Acts and Laws of Connecticut, 1784,* pp. 233-34.
14 *Revised Statutes of Connecticut, 1835,* Title 53.
15 *Acts and Laws of Massachusetts, 1783-1789,* p. 439; *The Public Laws of the State of Rhode Island and Providence Plantations, January, 1789,* p. 483. See James T. Adams, "Disfranchisement of Negroes in New England," *American Historical Review,* XXX (1925), 546.
16 *Acts and Laws of Massachusetts, 1787,* XXI.
17 *Hobbs et al. v. Fogg,* 6 Watt's Cases 553 (Pennsylvania Supreme Court, 1837).
18 Kirk H. Porter, *A History of Suffrage in the United States of America* (Chicago: University of Chicago Press, 1918), p. 90.

denying them the right to vote in state elections.[19] Everywhere in the North the condition of the free Negro worsened as slavery passed from the scene. "Thus it is," observed De Tocqueville, "that the prejudice which repels Negroes seems to increase in proportion as they are emancipated."[20]

Party politics after 1800 abetted the growth of virulent racism in the North. From the election of Jefferson until the Civil War the slave power of the South reached into the party councils of every state. The full weight of the slave states went to Jefferson in 1800. Jefferson received thirty-seven electoral votes from Virginia, South Carolina, Georgia, and Kentucky, and ten of them were derived from the slave population under the three-fifths rule. Those ten votes constituted the margin of victory over Adams and demonstrated conclusively where the balance of political power lay. Slaveholders thereafter provided the leadership of the Jeffersonian and Democratic parties. Entrenched in Congress and in the Electoral College, they wielded the lever of federal patronage in every state. Their power was so great that they were not only tolerated by their northern allies, they were patronized, flattered, and allowed to dictate. After 1800 the management of party affairs was in the hands of slaveholders, and every northern politician came to terms with this fact of political life.[21]

Because the principal concern of the South was the protection of slavery, northern party leaders were careful not to give any offense on this issue. Some went even further than the needs of party harmony required and

19 *The Public Laws of the State of Rhode Island and Providence Plantations, 1822,* pp. 89-90.

20 Alexis De Tocqueville, *Democracy in America* (New York: Colonial Press, 1900), I, 365.

21 Dumond, *Antislavery,* pp. 71-73.

deliberately stoked the fires of racial hatred in their own states. Anti-Negro demagoguery led to numerous disorders in which Negroes were beaten, brutalized, and sometimes killed by gangs of ruffians.[22] Riots occurred in Philadelphia at irregular intervals from 1829 to 1849.[23] Racial antagonism was kept at fever pitch by scurrilous pamphleteers who spewed forth a steady stream of anti-Negro invective. Probably the worst of the racist propagandists was the New York City pamphleteer John Jacobus Flournoy, who published virulent attacks on Negroes as a subhuman species, the enemies of all humanity and civilization.[24] In July 1834 one of the longest riots on record erupted in New York City. Hundreds of Negro homes were destroyed, and order was not restored until the governor sent troops into the city.[25] Northern politicians remained silent in the face of such outrages. But worse still, some actually abetted the rioters with the vilest sort of racial demagoguery. Thus they served the interests of their southern allies and maintained their own positions within the party.[26]

Northern politicians often had their own reasons for playing the racist game. In New York the Jeffersonian Republicans encouraged anti-Negro bias for local political advantage during the same years slavery was in the process of being extinguished. Gratitude to those members of the upper class who were prominent in the emancipation movement brought many Negro voters into politics as supporters of Federalism. The

---

22 Steward, *Twenty Years a Slave*, pp. 125, 167. See also Turner, *The Negro in Pennsylvania*, pp. 143-68.

23 Dumond, *Antislavery*, p. 219.

24 John Jacobus Flournoy, *An Essay on the Origin, Habits, etc., of the African Race: Incidental to the Propriety of Having Nothing to Do with Negroes; Addressed to the Good People of the United States* (New York, 1835), pp. 2-7. Cited in Dumond, *Antislavery*, p. 229.

25 Dumond, *Antislavery*, pp. 218-19.

26 *Ibid.*

close identification of many Federalist leaders, such as Hamilton, Jay, and Schuyler, with antislavery was evidence enough for Negroes that men such as these should be supported with the ballot. Although Negroes constituted only a small part of the electorate, their consistent support of Federalist candidates made them a formidable voting bloc. In several closely contested elections in the early nineteenth century their votes constituted the Federalists' margin of victory.[27]

Republican leaders in turn made a political issue of the Negro vote. They worked hard to discredit the Federalists with the white working class by depicting Federalism as the party of the Negro. In the election of 1808 the Republicans lyricized their racial venom in a campaign song which began "Federalists with blacks unite."[28] Republican watchers at the polls attempted to reduce the Negro vote by challenging every Negro who could not offer proof of his freedom.[29] Anti-Negro prejudice eventually became a test of party regularity for the New York Republican party. In 1815 the Republican-controlled legislature passed a law requiring Negroes to obtain special passes in order to vote in state elections.[30] Finally, in 1821 the Republicans successfully sponsored an amendment to the state constitution which increased the property qualification for voting from $100 to $250 for Negroes while abolishing it altogether for whites.[31] The effect of this amendment

27 Dixon Ryan Fox, *The Decline of Aristocracy in the Politics of New York* (New York: Columbia University Press, 1918), pp. 268-69.

28 Fox, "The Negro Vote in Old New York," *Political Science Quarterly*, XXXII (1917), 256-57.

29 *Ibid.*, p. 256.

30 *Ibid.*, p. 257.

31 This discriminatory provision remained in the New York Constitution until 1870, when the ratification of the Fifteenth Amendment made it violative of the United States Constitution. *Ibid.*, p. 262.

was to incorporate the concept of second-class citizenship for Negroes into the highest law of the state.

The concomitance of racism and the progress of emancipation posed a bitter problem not only for New York but for the North as a whole. Whites of the working class who rejected the Negro as a competitor under slavery were unwilling to accept him as an equal in free society. The racial polarization of the North which followed this act of class rejection was encouraged in turn by cynical politicians who used anti-Negro bias to gain the meanest sort of party advantage. Everywhere Negroes were shunned, cut off from free society, and excluded from most of the skilled occupations. Life held no promise for the Negro, for he was caught in a vise designed to crush and degrade him. Hemmed in by hostility and pilloried by demagogues, great numbers of Negroes sank to the level of pariahs condemned to a bitter existence on the fringe of free society.[32] There was no opportunity for them to develop their intellectual powers and no incentive for them to express their talents. Their isolation was complete. The Negroes were in a very real sense a population in quarantine, trapped in a system of racial bondage in many ways as cruel and intolerable as slavery.

[32] Steward, *Twenty-Two Years a Slave*, pp. 125, 167.

XI. THE MEANING
OF SLAVERY

W HY then did emancipation fall so short of giving the Negro real freedom, leaving him instead in what was really only another kind of bondage? There are no simple answers to this seminal tragedy of American history, but part of the answer can be found in the conceptual basis of the American slave system. Slavery in New York, as well as in the other English colonies, was based exclusively upon race. For 150 years first the Dutch and then the English equated bondage with color. In the statutes, local ordinances, port records, and census returns of the colonial era the word "Negro" was used interchangeably with "slave." The newspapers likewise used the words synonymously, for white New Yorkers took for granted the equation between race and slavery. The blanket enslavement of Negro prisoners of war during hostilities with Spain is a sharp reminder of what color meant in colonial times. That men should be slaves simply because they were Negro was a fact of life legitimized by law and accepted by most New Yorkers.

This invidious equation implied an inferiority of race which especially suited Negroes for slavery. That the whites came to accept this as the measure of the Negro raised a barrier between the two races that survived the slave system itself. In this regard the Dutch did not differ from the English. Slavery in New Netherland was racial in concept, and no attempt was ever made to put the system on anything but this simplistic basis. The Dutch treated their slaves well, but implicit in the system was the presumption of racial inferiority. The English simply took over the Dutch concept, though they sharpened its definition through legislation underscoring the alienation of the races.[1]

The principal difference between the English and the Dutch conceptions of slavery was that the latter regarded slavery as an important but not necessarily permanent system of labor. In New Netherland slavery was only a means to wealth for settlers who expected to return to Holland with their fortunes. Their easy-going attitude toward slave discipline was dictated not by humanity but by a lack of commitment to the colony as a permanent community.[2] The English, on the other hand, were committed to permanence, and this in turn required stronger measures of public control over all phases of colonial life. Thus the English legislated a series of regulations which transformed slavery from an essentially private to a public institution. These controls created separate systems of law and judicial procedure for slaves which gave slavery much sharper definition than it had under the Dutch.

In spite of the stricter controls imposed by the English, individual slaves continued to enjoy considerable freedom of action. They were able to hire their own time, accumulate property for their own use, reject prospective buyers, and even bargain with their masters for eventual freedom. That such conditions ex-

---

[1] In the Hispano-Portuguese colonies, where slavery had a legal rationale independent of race, this alienation of the races did not occur. See Frank Tannenbaum, *Slave and Citizen* (New York: Alfred A. Knopf, 1947), pp. 43-65, 92-113.

[2] In Guiana and Curaçao the Dutch were notoriously brutal masters. The lenity of the New Netherland slave system was the one bright spot on an otherwise dismal record. Elkins, *Slavery*, p. 77n.

isted can be credited to the expertise and determination of the slaves rather than the benevolence of the masters. Highly skilled slaves accounted for a large proportion of the slave force, and the need to obtain their cooperation compelled the master class to grant concessions. Slave workers in eighteenth-century New York mastered an array of technical skills unsurpassed in any other province. The occupational range of slavery paralleled free labor, and the slave therefore had some of the free worker's bargaining power in obtaining personal privileges from the master.

Such conditions produced a large number of aggressive slaves, secure in their skills and confident of their ability to bend the system to their individual needs. The New York bondsman had little in common with his Southern counterpart, whose initiative and talents were stultified by total domination under the plantation system. That the New York slave retained a personality and view of life peculiarly his own tends to support the thesis of Stanley M. Elkins that the complete subordination of the plantation slave to the control of the planter class annihilated his personality and "infantilized" his view of life to the extent that he assimilated the attitudes and values of the masters regardless of how invidious they were to himself or to his race.[3] The results were entirely different in New York, where the slaves were not only boldly self-assertive but often tenaciously pursued objectives which clashed with the interests of the masters.

The ability of slaves to bargain effectively with their masters considerably modified slavery over the years. In everyday practice the system had little resemblance to the master-slave relationship described in the regulatory statutes. For one thing, it was not mono-

[3] See Elkins, *Slavery*, pp. 103-15.

191

lithic; instead there were so many degrees of freedom within slavery that the latter lost much of its meaning as an absolute. Slavery held some bondsmen in a tighter grip than others, for individual slaves differed greatly in their ability to obtain concessions from the masters. The reality of slavery in a complex economic milieu was, in the phrase of Richard B. Morris, "a shadow zone of bondage" where conceptual absolutes had no practical meaning.[4]

New York slaves pushed this zone of bondage into the penumbra as they forced their way out of the shadows. What every slave desired most was freedom, and while only some could bargain for this directly, the continuous pressure by all slaves for minor concessions prepared the master class for the ultimate concession. The importance of manumission as an incentive to loyal service, as well as a safety valve against insurrection, was recognized by Governor Hunter in 1712 when he urged the legislature to encourage the practice.[5] The conditions under which slaves were usually freed—loyal service or payment of an agreed sum to the master or his heirs—make it clear that the bulk of the manumissions had little to do with philanthropy. Rather, manumission was the price that the master class paid for the efficient operation of the system.

Manumissions granted for purely economic reasons generated as powerful a force against slavery as the moralizing of the abolitionists. Every manumission undermined slavery, even when the slave bargained his way to freedom and the arrangement was made for the benefit of the master. This was so because every manumission was a clear admission that freedom was the

---

[4] See Morris, "The Measure of Bondage in the Slave States," *Mississippi Valley Historical Review*, XLI (1954), 219-40.
[5] *Supra*, pp. 142-43.

highest reward an owner could give to a slave. And this in turn implied that slavery was a form of racial punishment for those Negroes who were not set free. That Negroes as a group had done nothing to justify this punishment made the system morally indefensible. Thus even manumissions granted for selfish reasons under slave pressure undermined the system by underscoring its injustice. The ideology of antislavery was white, but the motive force pressing continuously for freedom was black.

The legal abolition of slavery likewise had economic concomitants, in this case a heavy influx of cheap white labor which changed the character of the working force. Census reports indicate that this trend started about two decades before statutory emancipation began. The gradual absorption of this stream of labor into the economy created a favorable climate for the antislavery idealism of the Revolutionary Era. This is not to say that idealism was not an important factor, only that it was not predominant. Although opponents of slavery stated the issue in ideological terms, the fact remains that no real progress was made toward general emancipation until the economy had virtually completed its adjustment to a system of free labor.

Although the emancipation statutes of 1799 and 1817 became effective on July 4, the ideological significance can be discounted as legislative hyperbole. Lawmakers have a penchant for putting their public acts, and of course themselves, in the best possible light. It is therefore not surprising that they wrapped their legislation in the mantle of idealism. It was much more high-minded after all to free the slaves because slavery was wrong than to free them because the system had become uneconomic. Yet the latter was the reality of emancipation, the former its rationalization. Slavery ended when it ceased to be profitable. Only then was the injustice of the system recognized and measures taken to implement emancipation.

Significantly abolitionists of the 1780's belonged to the business elite which thirty years before had reaped handsome profits from the slave trade. The precipitous decline of the trade after 1770 apparently sharpened the moral sensibilities of those who had formerly profited. It is not surprising that they directed their heaviest fire against the least profitable part of the system—the overseas slave trade, which by 1780 was already virtually extinct. The leaders of the abolition movement were honorable men who sincerely regarded slavery as a great moral wrong. But it is also true that they embraced antislavery at a time when it entailed no economic hardship for their class.

In the final analysis, the slave obtained his freedom only because his labor was no longer needed. As the profitability of slavery declined in the late eighteenth century, the system was abandoned as uneconomic by most users of labor. Thus statutory emancipation ratified the judgment already passed by the economy. It signalized the completion of New York's transition from increasingly expensive slave labor to a relatively cheap system of free labor. And because this transition was essentially a process of economic displacement, the tragedy of the Negro after emancipation becomes understandable. If idealism had been the motive force in the process, the Negro's reception into free society would have been different. The movement must be judged by its results, and the results for the Negro form a convincing body of evidence that emancipation was not designed to raise him to a better life but to displace him.

This displacement of the Negro was a visible feature of the emancipation movement. The anti-Negro riders which the Assembly tacked on to the emancipation bill of 1785 make it clear that the emancipators were not concerned with the welfare of the Negro. Their primary concern was to abolish slavery without disturbing the system of racial inequality upon which it rested. Those who supported emancipation on ideological grounds did nothing to prevent this. Once statutory emancipation was enacted, the schools and Negro charities supported by the upper class were neglected and eventually abandoned. These philanthropies were short-term projects which provided a useful forum against slavery, but they failed miserably to prepare the way for the Negro's meaningful participation in free society.

What happened to the Negro in New York after emancipation forms one of the darkest chapters in the history of the state. Emancipation did not bring real freedom; it brought only the exclusion of Negroes from the occupations and skills they had mastered under slavery. The slave system in New York was characterized by a high degree of specialization and division of labor which enabled Negro slaves to compete effectively with white workers. These skills were systematically destroyed after emancipation as Negroes were excluded from one occupation after another. Thus the Negro was deprived of what he had so painfully achieved under slavery: the opportunity and the ability to earn a livelihood for himself. The denouement for the Negro mocked the freedom which emancipation was expected to bring.

It is ironical that the struggle of the Negro for equal rights in the North today is largely a struggle to regain the place in the economy that he once occupied under slavery. The creation of a racially integrated labor force would hardly rank as an innovation, for full occupational mobility regardless of race existed in New York throughout the colonial era. Slavery did not prevent Negroes from acquiring economic expertise; rather, free society prevented them from using their skills and talents after emancipation. The end of slavery thus marked the beginning of a much more difficult journey for the Negro toward real emancipation. For the first freedmen this journey was hard and bitter, along a road heaped with the obstacles of implacable racial hostility. It has remained that way for their descendants, who are today the heirs and the voice of the promise that is America.

APPENDIX

DATA ON NEW YORK'S POPULATION, 1698-1790[1]

Counties	1698		1703	
	White	Negro[2]	White	Negro
Albany	1,453	23	2,015	200
Ulster and Dutchess	1,228	156	1,481	145
Orange	200	19	230	33
New York[3]	4,237	700	3,745	630
Richmond	654	73	407	97
Westchester	917	146	1,709	198
Suffolk	2,321	558	3,158	188
Kings	1,721	296	1,569	343
Queens	3,366	199	3,968	424
	15,897	2,170	18,282	2,258
	Total: 18,067		Total: 20,540[4]	

Counties	1723		1731	
	White	Negro	White	Negro
New York	5,886	1,362	7,045	1,577
Richmond	1,251	255	1,513	304
Kings	1,774	444	1,658	492
Queens	6,068	1,123	6,731	1,264
Suffolk	5,266	975	7,074	601
Westchester	3,961	448	5,341	692
Orange	1,097	147	1,785	184
Dutchess	1,040	43	1,612	112
Ulster	2,357	566	2,996	732
Albany	5,693	808	7,300	1,273
	34,393	6,171	43,055	7,231
	Total: 40,564		Total: 50,286	

[1] Statistics compiled from Greene and Harrington, *American Population before 1790*, pp. 92-105.

[2] The various census returns use the words "Negroes," "blacks" and "slaves" interchangeably.

[3] Note the heavy concentration of slaves in the New York City area at the beginning of the eighteenth century and the diffusion of the slave population after 1740.

[4] Plus 125 persons over the age of 60 unclassified by race.

	1737		1746	
Counties	White	Negro	White	Negro
New York	8,945	1,719	9,273	2,444
Albany	9,051	1,630	——	——
Westchester	5,894	851	8,563	672
Orange	2,547	293	2,958	310
Ulster	3,998	872	4,154	1,111
Dutchess	3,156	262	8,306	500
Richmond	1,540	349	1,691	382
Kings	1,784	564	1,686	645
Queens	7,748	1,311	7,996	1,644
Suffolk	6,833	1,090	7,855	1,399
	51,496	8,941	52,482	9,107

Total: 60,437   Total: 61,589[5]

	1749		1756	
Counties	White	Negro	White	Negro
New York	10,926	2,368	10,768	2,278
Kings	1,500	783	1,862	845
Albany	9,154	1,480	14,805	2,619
Queens	6,617	1,323	8,617	2,169
Dutchess	7,491	421	13,298	859
Suffolk	8,098	1,286	9,245	1,045
Richmond	1,745	409	1,667	465
Orange	3,874	360	4,456	430
Westchester	9,547	1,156	11,919	1,338
Ulster	3,804	1,006	6,605	1,500
	62,756	10,592	83,242	13,548

Total: 73,348   Total: 96,790

[5] Albany not included in census of 1746.

1771

Counties	Whites		Negroes	
	Males	Females	Males	Females
New York	9,083	9,643	1,500	1,637
Albany	20,698	18,131	2,226	1,651
Ulster	6,120	5,876	1,091	863
Dutchess	10,792	10,252	750	610
Orange	5,115	4,315	368	294
Westchester	9,566	8,749	1,777	1,653
Kings	1,268	1,193	606	556
Queens	4,286	4,458	1,156	1,080
Suffolk	5,912	5,764	798	654
Richmond	1,150	1,103	351	243
Cumberland	2,132	1,803	7	5
Gloucester	371	344	6	1
	76,493	71,631	10,636	9,247
	Total: 148,124		Total: 19,883	

Suffolk County Census, 1776

Townships	Whites		Negroes Male and Female
	Males	Females	
Shelter Island	69	72	33
St. George Manor and Meritches	135	157	84
Brookhaven	1,012	1,019	142
Southold	1,436	1,510	234
Smithtown	285	270	161
Easthampton	615	635	67
Islip	167	148	60
Southampton W.	666	695	61
Southampton E.	683	747	103
	5,068	5,253	945

Total Population: 11,266

199

1786

Counties	Whites		Negroes	
	Males	Females	Males	Females
Albany	34,933	32,737	2,335	2,355
Dutchess	15,810	15,181	830	815
Kings	1,384	1,285	695	622
Montgomery	7,393	7,259	217	188
New York	10,501	11,006	896	1,207
Orange	6,811	6,393	442	416
Queens	5,453	5,448	1,160	1,023
Richmond	1,281	1,178	369	324
Suffolk	6,392	6,333	567	501
Ulster	10,227	9,246	1,353	1,309
Washington	3,340	2,101	8	7
Westchester	9,940	9,364	649	601
	112,465	107,531	9,521	9,368
	Total: 219,996		Total: 18,889	

1790

Counties	Free Whites		Free Negroes	Slaves
	Male	Female		
Albany	37,415	34,407	170	3,929
Clinton	903	678	16	17
Columbia	13,310	12,744	55	1,623
Dutchess	22,030	20,940	440	1,856
Kings	1,603	1,414	46	1,432
Montgomery	15,058	13,152	41	588
New York	14,407	15,254	1,101	2,369
Ontario	716	342	6	11
Orange	8,940	8,371	201	966
Queens	6,417	6,480	808	2,309
Richmond	1,500	1,449	127	759
Suffolk	7,029	7,187	1,126	1,098
Ulster	13,849	12,485	157	2,906
Washington	7,358	6,625	3	47
Westchester	11,207	10,958	357	1,419
	161,742	152,486	4,654	21,329

Total Population: 340,211

BIBLIOGRAPHICAL NOTE

The manuscript collection of the New-York Historical Society contains a comparatively large proportion of the unpublished sources used in this study. Among the diaries, personal correspondence, and business records which contain information on the operation of slavery, the following are the most important: the Bancker Papers, Beekman Papers, De Peyster Papers, Warren Papers, and the letter books of Robert Cambridge Livingston and Jacobus Van Cortlandt. Information on the costs of slave maintenance, hiring rates, and the economics of slaveholding in general can be found in the accounts and ledgers of Hendrick Denker, William Faulkner, Johannes Lansing, Charles Nicoll, John Pryor, Elizabeth Schuyler, Benjamin Snyder, Abraham Wendell, and Thomas Witter.

Other useful manuscript sources in the New-York Historical Society are Francis L. Hawks' transcripts of the records of the Protestant Episcopal Church (much of the Hawks material is presently in the Church Historical Society, Austin, Texas), the minutes of the New York Manumission Society, and Daniel Parish's Transcripts of Material on Slavery in the Public Records Office in London. The Hawks transcripts contain letters from Anglican missionaries to the Society for the Propagation of the Gospel in Foreign Parts which describe the efforts made to proselytize the slaves. The minutes of the New York Manumission Society contain much valuable information on the organization, leadership, and tactics of the emancipation movement. Parish's transcripts are an indispensable source on several aspects of the slave system, especially the slave trade and problems of slave control. A good deal of general information can be found in six boxes of miscellaneous slavery manuscripts covering a wide range of topics.

A History of Negro Slavery in New York

Valuable material dealing with slavery on Long Island, particularly the eastern part of the island, is in the manuscript collection of the East Hampton Free Library. The most useful items are the account books of John Lyon Gardiner, Gardiner's Book of Colours or Mulatto Book, the Documents Book, and the Manuscript Scrapbook. Another useful collection of miscellaneous slavery manuscripts is in the Museum of the City of New York. Receipts, accounts, inventories, bills of sale, and manumission agreements contain information on the buying and selling of slaves and on the conditions under which slaves were manumitted. With regard to the latter, the Museum's manuscript Register of Manumissions is especially valuable.

An excellent collection of manuscript material relating to slavery is in the Historical Documents Collection of the Paul Klapper Library at Queens College of the City University of New York. The Klapper collection is relatively new, but it contains one of the best collections of the public records of colonial New York available anywhere. These include the records of the Justices Court and the Court of Sessions and Common Pleas of Ulster County, the Magistrates Court of Kingston, the Court of Chancery, the Mayor's Court of New York City, the Supreme Court of Judicature, and the Court of General Sessions. These records contain valuable information on judicial procedures relating to slavery, the enforcement of the slave controls, and crimes committed by slaves, as well as by whites, with respect to slavery.

For the New Netherland period of this book, there are several printed collections of primary material, among which the following are indispensable: E. B. O'Callaghan and Berthold Fernow, eds., *Documents Relative to the Colonial History of the State of New York,* 15 vols. (Albany: Weed, Parsons & Co., 1856–87); E. B. O'Callaghan, ed., *Laws and Ordinances of New Netherland, 1638–1674* (Albany: Weed, Parsons & Co., 1868); O'Callaghan, ed., *Calendar of Historical Manuscripts in the Office of the Secretary of State,* 2 vols. (Albany: Weed, Parsons & Co., 1866), Vol. I;

and O'Callaghan, ed., *Voyage of the Slavers St. John and Arms of Amsterdam* (Albany: J. Munsell, 1867). The latter contains much useful information on the slave trade. Also important are: Berthold Fernow, ed., *Minutes of the Orphanmasters Court of New Amsterdam*, 2 vols. (New York: Francis P. Harper, 1907); Fernow, ed., *Records of New Amsterdam, 1653–1674,* 7 vols. (New York: The Knickerbocker Press, 1897), which contains the minutes of the Court of Burgomasters and Schepens from 1653 to 1674; A. J. F. Van Laer, ed., *Correspondence of Jeremias Van Rensselaer, 1651–1674* (Albany: University of the State of New York, 1932); A. J. F. Van Laer and Jonathan Pearson, eds., *Early Records of the City and County of Albany and Colony of Rensselaerswyck,* 4 vols. (Albany, 1915–19); A. J. F. Van Laer, ed., *Minutes of the Court of Fort Orange and Beverwyck, 1652–1660,* 2 vols. (Albany: University of the State of New York, 1920–23); Van Laer, ed., *Minutes of the Court of Rensselaerswyck, 1648–1652* (Albany: University of the State of New York, 1922); and Van Laer, ed., *The Van Rensselaer Bowier Manuscripts* (Albany: University of the State of New York, 1908). The Van Rensselaer collections not only provide information on the role of slavery on the patroonship, but also offer many valuable details of the system in New Netherland as a whole.

Other primary sources for the New Netherland period are: Edward T. Corwin, ed., *Ecclesiastical Records of the State of New York,* 7 vols. (Albany: James B. Lyon Co., 1901–16), Vol. I of which contains useful information on master-slave relations, and I. N. Phelps Stokes, ed., *The Iconography of Manhattan Island,* 6 vols. (New York: R. H. Dodd, 1915–28). Among the contemporary observers and writers who commented upon slavery are the following: David De Vries, *My Third Voyage to America and New Netherland,* in New-York Historical Society, *Collections,* Ser. 2, III (1857); Cornelis Melyn, *Broad Advice to the United Netherland Provinces: or Dialogues about the Trade of the West India Company,* in New-York Historical Society, *Collections,* Ser. 2, III (1857); and A. Vanderhook,

A History of Negro Slavery in New York

Description of New Netherland, in New-York Historical Society, Collections, Ser. 2, III (1857). Other useful firsthand accounts can be found in J. Franklin Jameson, ed., Narratives of New Netherland, 1609–1664 (New York: Charles Scribner's Sons, 1909). For the legal theories underlying the New Netherland slave system, there are two valuable contemporary treatises on Roman-Dutch law in the seventeenth century: Ulric Huber, The Jurisprudence of My Time, tr. by Percival Gane, 2 vols. (London: Butterworth & Co., Ltd., 1939) and Dionysius Van der Keessel, Select Theses on the Laws of Holland and Zeeland, tr. by Charles A. Lorenz (London: Edward Stanford, 1855).

Of the sources used for the period after 1664, the colonial newspapers were especially valuable. Press coverage of slavery in the eighteenth century was particularly good and its importance for economic and social data relating to the institution cannot be stressed too strongly. Advertisements dealing with slaves for hire and sale and newpaper reports dealing with master-slave relations, the price of slaves, and the occupational range of slavery are a rich storehouse of information on virtually every aspect of the system. Among the papers used in this study, the following are the most important: Frothingham's Long Island Herald (1791–1798); the New York Gazette (1726–1734); Weyman's New York Gazette (1759–1767); the New York Gazetteer (1783–1787); the New York Independent Reflector (1752–1753); the New York Journal & Patriotic Register (1794–1800); the New York Journal and State Gazette (1784–1786); the New York Mercury (1752–1783); the New York Morning Post (1783); the New York Packet (1788); the New York Pacquet (1763); the New York Weekly Journal (1734–1743); the New York Weekly Post-Boy (1743–1773); The Farmer's Oracle (1797–1798); The Independent Journal (1783–1784); The Independent New York Gazette (1783–1784); The Poughkeepsie Journal (1789–1796); and The Royal Gazette (1779–1782). The most complete files of these papers are in the New-York Historical Society. These files are the starting point for any study of slavery in New York.

204

BIBLIOGRAPHICAL NOTE

For the laws, ordinances, and judicial decisions relating to slavery, the essential material can be found in the following: *Calendar of Council Minutes, 1668–1783* (Albany, 1902); Helen T. Catterall, ed., *Judicial Cases Concerning American Slavery and the Negro*, 5 vols. (Washington: Carnegie Institute, 1926–37); *Colonial Laws of New York from 1664 to the Revolution*, 5 vols. (Albany: James B. Lyon Co., 1894); *Journal of the Legislative Council of the Colony of New York, 1691–1775* (Albany: T. Weed, 1861); *Minutes of the Supreme Court of Judicature, 1673–1701*, in New-York Historical Society, *Collections*, XLV (1912); E. B. O'Callaghan, ed., *Calendar of Historical Manuscripts in the Office of the Secretary of State*, 2 vols. (Albany: Weed, Parsons & Co., 1866), Vol. II; *Proceedings of the General Court of Assizes, 1680–1682*, in New-York Historical Society, *Collections*, XLV (1912); and O'Callaghan and Fernow, eds., *Documents Relative to the Colonial History of the State of New York*, already cited. The *Minutes of the Common Council of the City of New York, 1675–1776*, 8 vols. (New York: Dodd, Mead & Co., 1905) contain material on the special problems of slave control in New York City. Valuable information on judicial procedure and slavery in the period immediately after the English occupation can be found in A. J. F. Van Laer, ed., *Minutes of the Court of Albany, Rensselaerswyck and Schenectady, 1668–1680*, 2 vols. (Albany: University of the State of New York, 1926–28).

Town records contain a vast amount of documentary material. Among the most useful for this study were the following: the *Brookhaven Town Records*, 2 vols. (New York, 1880–93); *Southold Town Records*, 2 vols., edited by J. Wickham Case (New York: S. W. Green's Sons, 1882–84); *Oyster Bay Town Records*, 2 vols., edited by John Cox (New York: Tobias A. Wright, 1916, 1924); *East Hampton Town Records*, 5 vols. (Sag Harbor: John S. Hunt, 1887–1905); *Records of the Town of New Rochelle*, edited by Jeanne A. Forbes (New Rochelle, 1916); *Hempstead Town Records*, 5 vols. (Jamaica, 1876–1901); *Jamaica Town Rec-*

ords (New York: Long Island Historical Society, 1914); *Records of the Town of Smithtown,* edited by William S. Pelletreau (Huntington: Long Islander Print, 1898); *Southampton Town Records,* 4 vols. (Sag Harbor: John S. Hunt, 1874–78); and *Huntington Town Records,* 3 vols., edited by Charles R. Street (Huntington: Long Islander Print, 1887–89). Other important local material can be found in Dixon Ryan Fox, ed., *Minutes of the Court of Sessions, 1657–1696, Westchester County* (White Plains: Westchester County Historical Society, 1924); Joel Munsell, ed., *Annals of Albany,* 10 vols. (Albany: J. Munsell, 1859); and Munsell, ed., *Collections on the History of Albany,* 4 vols. (Albany: J. Munsell, 1865).

The best published official sources on the slave trade are W. Noel Sainsbury, *et al.,* eds., *Calendar of State Papers: Colonial Series, America and West Indies,* 42 vols. (London: H.M.S.O., 1860–1953), an essential work abstracting most of the relevant British documents; W. L. Grant and James Munro, eds., *Acts of the Privy Council: Colonial Series, 1613–1783,* 6 vols. (London: Wyman & Sons, Ltd., 1908–12); and Elizabeth Donnan, ed., *Documents Illustrative of the Slave Trade to America,* 3 vols. (Washington: Carnegie Institute, 1930–35). Material on the vice-admiralty courts' condemnation of Negro prisoners of war as prize property can be found in Charles M. Hough, ed., *Reports of Cases in the Vice Admiralty of the Province of New York and the Court of Admiralty of the State of New York, 1715–1788* (New Haven: Yale University Press, 1925). Much useful information on the internal slave trade and the litigation arising from slave transactions is in Richard B. Morris, ed., *Select Cases of the Mayor's Court of New York City, 1674–1784* (Washington: The American Historical Association, 1935). Material on the participation of the merchant class in the slave traffic can be found in the *Letter Book of John Watts, 1762–1765,* in New-York Historical Society, *Collections,* LXI (1928). The files of the colonial newspapers already cited, particularly the *New York Weekly Post-Boy* and the *New York Mercury,* are a gold mine of information on every aspect of the trade. For master-slave relations and the everyday operation of slavery, much useful information can be found in the *Letters and Papers of Cadwallader Colden, 1711–1775,* 9 vols., in New-York Historical Society, *Collections,* L–LVI, LXVII–LXVIII (1917–23, 1934–35); *Papers of the Lloyd Family of the Manor of Queens Village,* 2 vols., in New-York Historical Society, *Collections,* LIX–LX (1926–27); and *Revolutionary and Miscellaneous Papers,* 3 vols., in New-York Historical Society, *Collections,* XI–XIII (1878–80). Material on the proselytizing activities of the Society for the Propagation of the Gospel is in the already cited collection of *Ecclesiastical Records* edited by Edward T. Corwin. For data on the ratio of Negro slaves to free whites, the best source is Evarts Greene and Virginia Harrington, *American Population before the Federal Census of 1790* (New York: Columbia University Press, 1932). Additional information on the slave population can be found in a compilation issued by the United States Census Bureau, *A Century of Population Growth in the United States, 1790–1900* (Washington: Government Printing Office, 1909), edited by W. A. Rossiter.

An invaluable source for material on private emancipation is *Abstracts of Wills on File in the Surrogate's Office,* 17 vols., in New-York Historical Society, *Collections,* XXV–XLI (1893–1913). The *Abstracts* contain a wealth of information on the incidence of manumission and the conditions under which it was granted. Besides the manuscript material already listed, additional data can be found in William S. Pelletreau, ed., *Early Wills of Westchester County* (New York: Francis P. Harper, 1898). The legal complications arising from manumission agreements between masters and slaves can be found in 1 Cowen, *New York Supreme Court Reports* (1832); 1 Athon, *New York Nisi Prius Reports* (1808); and 5, 14 Johnson, *New York Common Law Reports* (1810, 1817).

Several contemporary personal accounts are useful for their information on a wide range of topics. One of the best of these is by Anne Grant, *Memoirs of an American Lady,* 2 vols. (New York: Dodd, Mead & Co., 1901), which outlines the daily life of the slave and master-slave relations in the Albany area in the mid-eighteenth century. Daniel Horsmanden's *The New York Conspiracy: History of the Negro Plot, 1741–1742* (New York: Southwick & Pelsue, 1810) is a firsthand account of the conspiracy panic of 1741 by the judge who presided at the trials. Although biased and self-serving in the extreme, Horsmanden gives a number of valuable details about the trials as well as insight into the psychological impact of the affair on the whites. An interesting account of slavery and freedom from the standpoint of an ex-slave can be found in Austin Steward's *Twenty-Two Years a Slave and Forty Years a Freeman* (Rochester: William Alling, 1857). Henry Wansey's *An Excursion to the United States of America in the Summer of 1794* (Salisbury: J. Easton, 1798) describes the decline of slavery in New York City in the 1790's. An interesting account of the effort made to proselytize the slaves is in David Humphreys, *An Account of the Endeavours Used by the Society for the Propagation of the Gospel in Foreign Parts to Instruct the Negro Slaves in New York* (New York, 1730).

The impact of the Revolution on slavery is well documented. The best sources for the war years are V. H. Paltsits, ed., *Minutes of the Commissioners for Detecting and Defeating Conspiracies in the State of New York* (Albany: University of the State of New York, 1909–10); *Minutes of the Albany Committee of Correspondence, 1775–1778,* 2 vols. (Albany: University of the State of New York, 1923–25); and *Minutes of the Schenectady Committee of Correspondence* (included in Vol. II of the *Albany Minutes*). Useful information on the involvement of slaves on one side or the other can be found in the personal account of August Schlozer, *Briefwechsel,* 10 vols. (Göttingen: Vandenhoek, 1780–82), a Hessian officer under Burgoyne; the *Journal of Lieutenant Charles Philip Von Krafft, of the Regiment of Von Bose, 1776–1784,* in New-York Historical Society, *Collections,* XL (1882); and the *Proceedings of a*

*Board of General Officers of the British Army at New York,
1781,* in New-York Historical Society, *Collections,* XLIX
(1916). The statutory suppression of slavery after the war
can be traced in the *Journals of the New York Provincial
Congress,* 2 vols. (Albany, 1842); *Public Laws of the State of
New York* (Albany, 1781–1800); *Journals of the Assembly
of the State of New York* (Albany, 1785–1800); and *Journals
of the Senate of the State of New York* (Albany, 1785–1800).

Among the secondary sources, there is no satisfactory
general work on slavery in New York. The only published
work presently available is Ansel J. Northrup's *Slavery in
New York* (Albany: University of the State of New York,
1900), a loose conspectus with many deficiencies, of which
the most serious is a complete lack of documentation. The
best secondary coverage of the subject can be found in
Samuel McKee, *Labor in Colonial New York, 1664–1776*
(New York: Columbia University Press, 1935), a highly
readable, thoroughly researched work, though mainly economic in focus. Other studies which provide a variety of
topical information are by Leo H. Hirsch, Jr., "The Negro
in New York, 1783–1865," *Journal of Negro History,* XV
(1931); Henry H. Ingersoll, "The New York Plot of 1741,"
The Green Bag, XX (1908); A. G. Lindsay, "The Economic
Condition of the Negroes of New York prior to 1861,"
Journal of Negro History, VI (1917); Henry McCloskey,
"Slavery on Long Island," *Brooklyn Common Council Manual* (1864); Edgar J. McManus, "Antislavery Legislation in
New York," *Journal of Negro History,* XLVI (1961); Aaron
H. Payne, "The Negro in New York prior to 1860," *How-
ard Review,* I (1923); C. E. Pierre, "The Work of the So-
ciety for the Propagation of the Gospel in Foreign Parts
among the Negroes of the Colonies," *Journal of Negro
History,* XIII (1928); and William L. Stuart, "Negro Slavery in New Jersey and New York," *Americana,* XVI (1922).

Much useful material, some of it documentary, can
be found in the huge, though uneven, compilation by
David T. Valentine, *Manual of the Corporation of the City
of New York,* 28 vols. (New York: Francis P. Harper, 1900).

A History of Negro Slavery in New York

For the New Netherland period, there are J. H. Innes, *New Amsterdam and Its People* (New York: Charles Scribner's Sons, 1902) and Ellis Raesly, *Portrait of New Netherland* (New York: Columbia University Press, 1945), both careful, scholarly works containing pertinent background information. An early work that continues to be useful is E. B. O'Callaghan's *History of New Netherland*, 2 vols. (New York: D. Appleton & Co., 1855). For the activities of the Society for the Propagation of the Gospel, the best secondary source is Ernest Hawkins, *Historical Notices of the Missions of the Church of England in the North American Colonies, Previous to the Independence of the United States: Chiefly from the MS. Documents of the Society for the Propagation of the Gospel in Foreign Parts* (London: B. Fellowes, 1845). Additional information can be found in Morgan Dix, *A History of the Parish of Trinity Church in the City of New York*, 5 vols. (New York: The Knickerbocker Press; Columbia University Press, 1898–1950). For the slave trade, there are W. E. B. Du Bois, *The Suppression of the African Slave Trade to the United States of America, 1638–1870* (New York: Longmans, Green & Co., 1904), John H. Spears, *The American Slave Trade* (New York: Charles Scribner's Sons, 1901), and Kenneth G. Davies, *The Royal African Company* (New York: Longmans, Green & Co., 1957); also useful are Albert A. Giesecke's *American Commercial Legislation before 1789* (Philadelphia: University of Pennsylvania, 1910) and Klaus E. Knorr, *British Colonial Theories* (Toronto: University of Toronto, 1944). A good deal of interesting information on fugitive slaves can be found in Kenneth W. Porter, "Relations between Negroes and Indians," *Journal of Negro History*, XVII (1932).

The impact of the Revolution on slavery is described in several books and articles, among which the following are the most useful: Benjamin Quarles, *The Negro in the American Revolution* (Chapel Hill: University of North Carolina Press, 1961); William C. Nell, *The Colored Patriots of the Revolution* (Boston, 1855); and W. B. Hartgrove, "The Negro Soldier in the American Revolution,"

BIBLIOGRAPHICAL NOTE

Journal of Negro History, I (1916). For the emancipation movement and its political concomitants in the North in the late eighteenth century, the best secondary account is in Dwight L. Dumond's admirable *Antislavery: The Crusade for Freedom in America* (Ann Arbor: University of Michigan Press, 1961). The town and county histories cited in the notes, particularly J. Thomas Scharf's *History of Westchester County,* 2 vols. (Philadelphia: L. E. Preston & Co., 1886) and Jeptha R. Simms, *History of Schoharie County and Border Wars of New York* (Albany: Munsell & Tanner, 1845), were useful at numerous points in this study.

For the institutional setting, an indispensable work is Richard B. Morris' classic *Government and Labor in Early America* (New York: Columbia University Press, 1946), which contains an immensity of information on the whole colonial labor scene. Material on the legal foundations of slavery can be found in Thomas R. R. Cobb, *An Inquiry into the Law of Slavery in the United States of America* (Philadelphia: T. Johnson & Co., 1858); William Goodell, *The American Slave Code* (New York, 1853); John C. Hurd, *The Law of Freedom and Bondage in the United States,* 2 vols. (Boston: Little, Brown & Co., 1858–62), Vol. I of which contains abstracts of the slave codes of each colony; George M. Stroud, *A Sketch of the Laws in Relation to Slavery in the United States of America* (Philadelphia: Kimber & Sharpless, 1827); and Jacob D. Wheeler, *Practical Treatise on the Law of Slavery* (New York, 1837). The best secondary source on the slave statutes and the judicial procedures of slavery is by Julius Goebel and T. Raymond Naughton, *Law Enforcement in Colonial New York* (New York: Columbia University, 1944), a scholarly, encyclopedic work that explores the whole spectrum of this intricate subject; also useful is Edwin Olson's "The Slave Code in Colonial New York," *Journal of Negro History,* XXIX (1944). For the transformation of New York's economy in the late eighteenth century and the transition from slavery to a system of free labor, E. Wilder Spaulding's

211

New York in the Critical Period (New York: Columbia University Press, 1932) is indispensable.

The general setting of the subject is described in several standard works, of which the most useful is John H. Franklin's *From Slavery to Freedom* (New York: Alfred A. Knopf, 1963), a meticulous, scholarly work containing a storehouse of information on the Negro in the colonial period. Also useful are the studies of John W. Cromwell, *The Negro in American History* (Washington: American Negro Academy, 1914); Charles S. Johnson, *The Negro in American Civilization* (New York: Henry Holt & Co., 1930); and Carter G. Woodson, *The Education of the Negro prior to 1861* (New York: G. P. Putnam's Sons, 1915). Despite interpretative shortcomings, Ulrich B. Phillips' *American Negro Slavery* (New York: D. Appleton & Co., 1918) is still a valuable source of solid information on the origins of the American slave system. Finally, there are two general works that no student of slavery can afford to ignore. Kenneth Stampp's *The Peculiar Institution* (New York: Alfred A. Knopf, 1956), to which I am deeply indebted for many insights, is the authoritative statement on the subject. Stanley M. Elkins' brilliant *Slavery* (New York: Grosset & Dunlap, 1961) not only throws new light on slavery as a problem of historiography but is a fine example of how an interdisciplinary approach can bring old problems into new focus.

212

INDEX

215

INDEX

Testimony, slave: accepted in court, 18, 79; not accepted, 80
Thatcher, Thomas: required to prove ownership of alleged slave, 61
Thomson, Charles: denounces slavery, 153
Thorne, James, 144
Tocqueville, Alexis de: on racial prejudice in the North, 185
Tories: encourage slave desertions, 155-56
Trade. *See* Slave trade
Trumbull, Jonathan (Governor), 155

Ury, John: accused in Negro Plot, 133-36

Valloau, Steven: fined for trading with slaves, 83
Van Dam, Rip: on slave imports, 35
Van Rensselaer, Kiliaen: orders slaves used against white tenants, 17

Vermont: slavery abolished in, 118, 181-82
Ver Planck, Philip, 46
Vice-Admiralty Court: Negro prisoners of war sold into slavery by, 87-89

Washington, George: on slavery, 152; on enlisting Negroes in the Continental Army, 157
Watts, John, 39
Wells, Obadiah, 31
Wilson, Christopher: questioned about Hogg burglary, 126-27
Woolman, John, 152
Working class: attitude toward slavery, 183-84; anti-Negro prejudice of, 188

York, Duke of: supports the slave trade, 23

Zenger, John Peter: on slavery, 151